Presidential Candidate Patrick Anthony Ockander:

Defending Our Constitution and Restoring Power to the People

2016

LET FREEDOM RING!

By:

Patrick Anthony Ockander

This book is dedicated to you, the Reader and,

To all Medics,

To the Honorable Men and Women of 1/23 Infantry

And to all our Service Men and Women of today and yesterday

To ALL people everywhere who share, respect, protect, propagate, and defend Truth, Love, Light, Families, Freedom, Wisdom, History, and Knowledge,

To ALL PATRIOTS EVERYWHERE, and EVERYWHEN,

To my Brothers and Sisters,

To the two most important Women in my Life:

My beautiful wife Kathryn Nicole Ockander,
My amazing mother, Virginia Carol Ockander,

And, I further extend my dedication of this book to three Men who I highly esteem:

1. Glenn Beck
2. David Barton
3. & My Father, Kenneth Wayne Ockander

I do thank you, and dedicate this Effort. God Bless You All.

PLEDGE OF ALLEGIANCE

I, Patrick Anthony Ockander, do hereby pledge my allegiance to the flag, of the United States of America, and to the Republic, for which it stands, One Nation, under GOD, indivisible, for Liberty and Justice for ALL.

Brothers and Sisters,

I'm running for the office of President of The United States of America. If you hire me for this job I promise to tell you the Truth in the face of adversity.

I intend to be the voice of The People.

I will always keep you fully informed of our nation's status, and warn you when danger lurks ahead.

I have listed the planks to my platform in front of my narrative, and ask that you understand that my positions and the solutions I've presented here are based upon the information I have available to me up to now.

When I am able to more fully assess each plank, from the perspective of sitting president, any changes that may need to be made will be directly worked out with you prior to taking any action, outside emergent situations.

I promise to perform the duties expected of Our Commander-In-Chief with the utmost respect for our nation, our Constitution, for you, and for the Executive office.

I will NOT let you down. May GOD Bless America, Now and Forever.
Thank you.

Sincerely, Patrick Anthony Ockander

Do not go gentle into that good night

By Dylan Thomas, 1914 - 1953

Do not go gentle into that good night,
Old age should burn and rave at close of day;
Rage, rage against the dying of the light.

Though wise men at their end know dark is right,
Because their words had forked no lightning they
Do not go gentle into that good night.

Good men, the last wave by, crying how bright
Their frail deeds might have danced in a green bay,
Rage, rage against the dying of the light.

Wild men who caught and sang the sun in flight,
And learn, too late, they grieved it on its way,
Do not go gentle into that good night.

Grave men, near death, who see with blinding sight
Blind eyes could blaze like meteors and be gay,
Rage, rage against the dying of the light.

THE PLATFORM:

MY PRESIDENTIAL MOTIVATIONS:

I, Patrick Anthony Ockander, am seeking the office of President of the United States of America. I have a strong desire to serve you, my Brothers and Sisters, my fellow Americans, in the spirit of Honesty, Constitutionalism, Justice, and Charity.

I seek this office out of a sincere desire to assist in restoring Our Freedom. I will not sit quietly, idly watching the systematic destruction of Our country We All Love so much, especially when there's something that can be done about it.

I am determined to be completely Honest with you, and I will do so with no forethought of personal cost, or if having already done so, will remain honest with you still.

I seek to return the power to the Citizens of America, We, The People, and hope to trigger a Great American Reunion, a Jubilee of debt forgiveness, a new treaty with our international neighbors, and seek to rescue the persecuted Christians and Jewish people in All Lands. We are all one big family. I believe it's well past time we start acting like one. We've got thousands, if not millions of suffering Christians and Jewish Men, Women and Children worldwide. Will you just sit idly by and not come to their rescue?

I am determined to not accept funding from big businesses in an effort to remain string-free—I recognize the powerful influence these contributions can make, however, I would ask that any businesses who truly desire to help me help U.S., I would ask them to please donate to the Nazarene Fund at www.mercuryone.org. Thank you. I Truly desire to represent the will of The People. I am determined to Earn your Trust and Hope that you help me get the job, and later to assist U.S. in the work.

Please register to vote, early, get others to register too, pray for Our Nation, for Israel, often, and please pray for me too, if you will.

While in office, I am seeking:

- To reform and reinforce our international alliances
- Debt elimination/forgiveness/jubilee
- The return to our core Constitutional values
- The expiration of frivolous, outdated, unnecessary, and "funny" laws
- The attachment of expiration dates on all new and existing laws.
- Freedom of conscience
- The preservation of LIFE
- An end to ethnic cleansing
- An informed and intelligent public
- Respect of American's right to privacy (end the Patriot Act).
- The undoing of political correctness

- Elimination of formal taxation, and the phasing out of the Federal Reserve.
- Better treatment and payment for our service-members
- Truth and accountability in politics, and of our politicians
- Freedom of information
- Purge of bureaucracy, especially of the EPA, FDA, NSA, and TSA
- Opt in and opt out waivers for mandatory healthcare
- Technological advancement with government restrictions removed
- Application of new energy sources/technologies
- Faster, cleaner, more efficient modes of transportation
- Intelligent traffic infrastructure that increases fuel efficiency, decreases travel times, and makes sense.
- Traffic penalty system that imposes driving restrictions rather than expensive fines and court costs.
- Revision of traffic laws, and application of common sense into our traffic infrastructure
- Reduce traffic fatalities
- Restoration of second amendment rights
- Increased wages for lower paid healthcare workers: Nurses, EMTs, Techs, and assistive personnel who are exposed to dangerous pathogens, unique physical and mental demands, and have been underpaid and under represented for too long.

- Seek to restore Nicolai Tesla's name in history, and implement many of his contributions to society, and incorporate many of his technologies that help to set men free
- Seek better education systems that are truthful, transparent, free of charge, and convenient, where parents take on a larger role in their children's educational development, and this education can be shared and strengthened through international cooperation.
- Removal of the position of tzars in America
- To get cops focused back on the job they were hired to do, and to stop the bullying and fear creation that they and media have inflicted on society in general.
- The elimination/reduction of corruption in government
- Internet freedom, and the removal of much of the regulations that have been imposed thus far, for example, net neutrality, and Internet taxation laws.
- Sensible laws
- Elimination of government fines and fees
- Restoration of Limitations of executive, judicial, and legislative powers, as constitutionally dictated.
- Change wage scale for all federally elected positions including president, house, and senate (to be based on the Annual Average American Individual Income AAAII across the board).
- Restoration of American values

- Honesty and accountability in media
- Recognition that America is founded on Christian values, and that America is, in fact, a Christian nation, with the God of Abraham at its helm (if We will recognize and worship Him).
- Decriminalization of drugs in general, and complete elimination of punishment for ingestion of any substance, toxic or not.
- Stop allowing agencies that seizes the property of others from directly profiting from it. No spoils to the government victors. Any proceeds from legal seizures need to go to 100% charitable organizations chosen from random lotteries, or distributed equally among all, or distributed to, or within the disenfranchised communities, or some other mode of distribution that We can all agree on. But this present practice must cease.
- Simplification of the immigration process, and a reduction in the cost to process individuals. Placement of Christian refugees first in line at Ellis Island (Our Golden Door).
- Work with Mexico to increase their standard of living and assist in reducing corruption in their government.
- Restoration of Ellis Island, it's purpose, use, personnel, and its infrastructure
- Provide regular informational firesides with Americans, where I can be directly interacted with, and questioned openly.

- Actively find those who have been unjustly imprisoned and offer them pardons, restitution, and employment assistance
- Debt forgiveness within the U.S.A. with the implementation of a Jubilee, and an extending offer to Our international community for participation as well.
- Increased acceptance of internships, apprenticeships, and on the job training.
- Creation of a pathway that converts life experience into a transcript format that is certifiable, easy to use, understandable, on par with educational degrees when applicable, and streamlined.
- Exercise patience with international community
- Extension of friendship to our international community
- Exercise extreme prejudice towards those who harm others, both within and without our nation.
- Creation of an "A-Team" (Department of Offense [DoO]) and a streamlining of the (Department of Defense [DoD]) "B-Team".
- Quick, accurate extermination of those who are the working hand of genocide, decapitations, enslavement, torture, rape of men, women and children, crucifixion, and other terrible atrocities.
- Freedom for Americans to refuse immunizations without retribution (truth in immunotherapy).

- An undoing of all of the nefarious, subversive actions taken against the American people and our Republic.
- I am seeking the assistance of every willing American who can help get the word out, and help get others registered to vote.
- Return to domestic tranquility
- Establish friendship within the international community
- Identification, containment of, and destruction of those who seek declare war on Israel, America, and Our Allies.
- It's time to get right with our maker and the ultimate Return to One Nation Under God.
- And of course, I am motivated to Help U.S. finally find Cures For Cancer (CFC) as well as many other serious conditions. Promote the common welfare.

MY PLANKS

~ In Alphabetical Order ~

1. ABORTION & INFANTICIDE
2. ANIMAL RIGHTS
3. ARMED FORCES MEMBER RIGHTS
4. ARMED FORCES PAY, QUALIFICATIONS, ETCETERA
5. AUTOMOTIVE TRAFFIC
6. BORDERS
7. CANCER
8. CENSORSHIP
9. CHILDREN & CHILDREN'S RIGHT TO PLAY (PURSUIT OF HAPPINESS)
10. CONSTITUTIONAL LAW ENFORCEMENT PROTECTIONS AGENCY (CLEPA)
11. CORRUPTION IN GOVERNMENT
12. DNA
13. ELECTROMAGNETIC PULSE (EMP) DEFENSES
14. ENERGY, OIL & OTHER
15. ENVIRONMENTAL PROTECTION AGENCY (EPA) & CAP AND TRADE
16. FAMILIES
17. FARMERS & FARMING / RANCHERS & RANCHING
18. FEDERAL GOVERNMENT MONEY MANAGEMENT
19. FEDERAL RESERVE / GOLD STANDARD / GOLD RESERVES
20. FOREIGN FINANCIAL AID / FOREIGN FUNDING
21. FOOD AND DRUG ADMINISTRATION (FDA)

22. FREEDOM OF SPEECH / PRESS
23. FRIEND? OR FOE?
24. HEALTHCARE
25. HEINOUS CRIMES & CRIMINALS
26. HIGHER EDUCATION
27. HOMEOWNER'S ASSOCIATIONS (HOAs)
28. HOME SCHOOLING / PARENT TEACHERS
29. HOSPITAL RIGHTS & RESPONSIBILITIES
30. HUMAN LIBERTIES (MANKINDS' LIBERTIES)
31. HUMAN RIGHTS
32. IMMIGRATION / CITIZENSHIP & NATURALIZATION
33. ILLEGAL IMMIGRATION / IMMIGRANTS
34. INCARCERATION and REHABILITATION
35. INCREASED WAGES / WAGES IN GENERAL
36. INDIVIDUAL RIGHTS
37. INTERNET
38. IRAN
39. ISRAEL
40. JUBILEE & DEBT ~ AMERICAN NATIONAL & FOREIGN DEBT
41. JUSTICE SYSTEM CORRUPTION
42. LAW ENFORCEMENT
43. LOCAL RIGHTS
44. MANDATORY HEALTH INSURANCE (OBAMACARE)
45. MARRIAGE ~ STRAIGHT, PLURAL, GAY & OTHER
46. MEDICARE
47. MILITARY
48. MOTHERS & CHILD REARING
49. NASA, DARPA, SKUNKWORKS, AREA 51
50. NEW WORLD ORDER

51. PATIENT RIGHTS & RESPONSIBILITIES
52. PATRIOT ACT
53. PERPETUAL EDUCATION
54. PERSONALLY OWNED VEHICLES & TRAFFIC
55. PERSONAL PROPERTY RIGHTS & RESPONSIBILITIES
56. PHYSICIAN RIGHTS & RESPONSIBILITIES
57. PLAN FOR SERVICE MEMBERS / DEPLOYMENTS / NATIONAL DEFENSE
58. PREGNANCY ASSISTANCE / RIGHT TO LIFE
59. PRISON SYSTEM
60. PRIVACY / SNOOPING
61. PROPANDA / PSYCHOLOGICAL OPERATIONS (PSY OPS) USAGE IN AMERICA
62. RACISM
63. RELIGION
64. RIGHT TO BE
65. RIGHT TO INGEST—DRUGS, FOOD, POISON
66. RIGHT TO LIFE
67. SECOND AMENDMENT
68. SECURITY
69. SEPARATION OF CHURCH AND STATE
70. SEX OFFENDERS / STRANGER KIDNAPPERS / PEDOPHILES
71. SMALL BUSINESS / NEW BUSINESS
72. SPORTS MEDICINE
73. SOCIAL SECURITY
74. SOCIAL SERVICES
75. STATES' RIGHTS
76. STOCK TRADING WHILE IN PUBLIC OFFICE

1.

ABORTION & INFANTICIDE

Right to Life:

- The Constitution recognizes humanity's Right to Life (Liberty and the Pursuit of Happiness) as protected and endowed by Our Creator. It is therefore within the scope of government to protect such life when it is threatened.

- Abortion existed at the time our forefathers wrote the Constitution, and our forefathers had something to say about it. They deemed abortion illegal, and recognized that life began at conception.

Federal Protections:

- Developing fetuses have the right to federal protection (from the point of conception, forward).

Outlaw Elective Abortions:

- Abortion is legal only in emergent, life-threatening situations, and as an option extended to victims of sexual crime under professional, spiritual and legal advise.

- PERMANENTLY SHUT DOWN the Planned Parenthood operation, other abortion mills, lone wolf operations, and remove the morning-after pill from market.

Creation of The Conception Connection:

- At the point of conception a pregnant female can go to her local court, initiate a request for transfer of parental rights to a suitable couple. The judge would assign a case number and representation to the unborn fetus would begin. Counseling would be provided throughout the pregnancy.

- Adoption will replace abortion.

- Options can include adoption, change of mind, or (future advances might offer transplantation of fetal life to a willing woman [adoptive parent] thereby creating a ("Conception Connection").

- Local judicial systems will absorb the costs associated with legal representation, and will take responsibility for all costs associated with this, and will render this service to society for perpetuity, out of respect of All Human Life, and in memorial of the millions of innocent lives lost to Abortion under our "modern" system.

The Future:

- As mentioned above, I believe there will be medical breakthroughs in the field zygote and fetal transplantation. At some point, transplantation of a fetus from one mother to another might be an option, but hopefully the need to utilize this method will be rare.

A Memorial:

- I suggest we create a memorial to all the children who lost their lives to abortion, as a constant reminder to U.S. of what we allowed to happen on Our Watch, of what was required to stop it, and how important it is that we never return to this immoral practice.

2.

ANIMAL RIGHTS

- Right to not be destroyed solely based on overpopulation of the kennel system—regarding our current situation of animal collection, and destruction

- Right to not suffer unnecessarily while being raised and when being slaughtered.

- Right to life, so long as that life does not come before the life or welfare of Humans.

- I support using our excessive number of animals in shelters to help rehabilitate individuals within our prison systems.

3.

ARMED FORCES MEMBER (AFM) RIGHTS

- Right to all Constitutional rights that are normally afforded to our citizens, within minimal necessary limitations for security, etc.

- Fair Pay; Pay worthy of the ultimate sacrifice all armed forces members face.
- Excellent Healthcare
- Good Food
- Good Learning Environment, with emphasis on Constitutional Ethics and Principles incorporated, daily.
- Healthy athletics, with the incorporation of proven dietary supplementation for increased physical strength and health.

- Extension of veteran benefits to spouses, as well as equality in pension benefits between the two married individuals (recognize the spouse is key to the success of our AFMs)

- Competent Leadership; when incompetency surfaces, AFMs have the Right to have their concerns with their leadership brought to the attention of the proper authority, judged, and corrected/addressed as needed. Put pride aside.

- Due to the incorporation of all sexes and sexualities, AFMs have the Right to private showers and private/secure housing when possible.

- Right, and expectation, to Keep and Bear Arms; Including On-Post, after passing initial training, peer review, and a psychological evaluation.
- Right to Drink, At Any Age, if enlisted or commissioned regardless of any national "Legal Age".
- Right to vote and have those votes counted, regardless of AFMs age, or duty location

- Right to grow facial hair (not all environments require immediate CBC precautions, and a man can shave his beard within minutes).

- Right to not have their belongings auctioned off in storage rental sell offs. This would be as a safeguard provided to All AFMs, in the event they are killed in action, delayed, captured, missing, or otherwise unable to secure their belongings when in the service to our nation. Their belongings would be protected, insured, and guaranteed by armed forces funding and representation.

4.

ARMED FORCES QUALIFICATIONS, STANDARDIZATIONS, FITNESS, BENEFITS, COMBAT ACTIONS

- Constitutional studies will be incorporated into all servicemen and servicewomen's training

- Service members will be expected to be the finest men and women available, meeting the highest qualifications, and therefore being financially rewarded at the highest-level We, The People can afford.
- Pay scale streamlined, and made equal to that of our congressmen (which will be equal to the national average income, during any given year) and increased 25% for those actively performing combat missions (based upon mission logs).
- All service members receive pensions, regardless of their time in service. However, pensions on-par with time in service, injuries sustained, awards received, and actual service rendered.
- Spouses of veterans to be counted as eligible for care within the VA, and pension is split between the two if/when divorcing.

- We will reduce the usage of our armed forces when possible
- Provide our service members with the best equipment, training, and arms available

- When our armed forces must be used, our action must be well thought out, direct, intense, and fully over-powering and destructive of the enemy.

- If enemy does not abide by the accepted laws of war (Geneva Conventions agreement), our service members cannot be expected to follow such requirements either.

- Each combat mission should be treated like a serious sports event (as far as preventive medicine goes) Therefore we must provide our service members with adequate and proper mental, spiritual, and physical preparation prior to engaging the enemy, regularly, and air condition their vehicles whenever possible.

- Treat service members as professional athletes when rendering their care.
- Incorporate sports medicine discipline and oversight during physical fitness, training, field exercises, and combat movements.

- Medics can be trained-up by sports medicine doctors and specialists to assist in wrapping ankles, knees, wrists, etc. (prior to combat and training).

- Healthcare benefits on par with our congressmen

5.

AUTOMOTIVE TRAFFIC

Problem:

Thousands of unnecessary fatalities on American Roadways

Solution:

- Widespread identification and removal of deadly obstacles (poles, walls, trees, missing dividers, parked cars, etc.) intersections, and roadways with an equally massive undertaking to correct the hazards on a national scale.
- Incentivize the placement of roundabouts over intersections that are often deadly, and also require expensive electronics and maintenance.
- Provide safe rides. Decrease alcohol related fatalities by establishing a network of towing/taxi services that provide safe transit for those under the influence.
- Alcohol producing companies, and establishments that profit from alcohol will be responsible for financing this responsibility
- National driver's license (that is recognized internationally) and is

non-RFID (radio frequency [emitting] Identification).

- Establish performance ratings that can be simplified and understood by all that would include vehicle's speed rating, tires, drivers proven ability, and other commonsense variables.

Problem:

Commuters are the target of what can be compared to a $hake-down. Through fines, fees, taxes, and penalties, law enforcement, and government agencies have been stealing from the pockets of Americans daily.

Solution:

- Reduce the ability for individuals to be harassed while in traffic.
- Streamline and reduce or remove traffic fines and punishments.
- Require safety departments to publicly disclose all fines imposed, daily.
- Protect consumers from wasteful revolving Department of Motor Vehicles (DMV) registration fees (yet another government $hakedown). One fee, once, if any.
- Eliminate practice of duplicate taxes being paid on a vehicle that has previously been taxed.

- National On-Line DMV that provides almost all the resources required, from the comfort of your home.
- Creation of National driver's license

Problem:

Wasted time, gasoline, life, and money stuck in traffic.

Solution:

- Support simple fixes that make everyone's lives more enjoyable, such as replacing two of the stop signs at a 4-way stop, with yield signs in the direction of heaviest traffic. Or redefining what a stop sign means altogether, maybe something like, "slow down to a safe enough speed that you are certain there's not oncoming or crossing traffic".
- Incorporate intelligence into our traffic-signal system. Systems set up to assist in optimum traffic flow, with fewer wasteful stops.
- Incorporate variable-speed lanes within large highway systems, allowing for faster travel to the left, and slower travel to the right.
- Less focus on speed, and more focus on safety.
- Create a national drivers license that would allow better drivers to drive with increased freedom.

- Drivers would be able to drive a higher rated vehicle, faster, if their personal rating allowed for it (with national DL).

6.

BORDERS

- We have the Right, and the Duty to Protect our Nation from enemy intrusion, especially now when the threat of domestic terror is so high.

- We need to Protect and support landowners who are presently under assault by illegal intrusion into our country.

- It's time we aggressively defend our borders and create an international atmosphere that creates less need to come into our country to begin with (help our southern neighbors help themselves).

- Suggest deploying our Armed Forces to the border to stop the immediate influx.

- Suggest the establishment of temporary/permanent military facilities along problem border areas.

- Deploy Handheld Interagency Identity Detection Equipment (HIIDE) (biometrics) to collect and classify, detain, deport, or retain individuals who are not legally residing in our nation.

- Put an end to the Anchor Baby pathway to citizenship flaw in our system.

7.

CANCER

- Spare no expense finding cures for Cancer.

8.

CENSORSHIP

- Outside the Department of Defense (DOD) I believe in nearly complete transparency within the federal government.

- Therefore, I believe the federal government should not be censoring information unless it is truly critical to our nations' security.

- I still support maintaining basic standards of decency within the public domain, whether real or virtual.

- All offensive Internet material can be cataloged within its own domain, and readily censored by the end-user. For example, pornography can be listed under .xxx, versus .com, and drug related content could be listed under something else.

- Set a government mandate to stop the intrusion into The People's viewing, reading, and entertainment choices.

9.

CHILDREN
&
RIGHT TO PLAY (PURSUIT OF HAPPINESS)

- The rights of our children, to grow and be happy, healthy individuals must be protected. Children need to be nurtured, lead, guided and directed by their parents as much as possible. More emphasis should be placed on learning within the home setting rather than outside in the public education realm.
- Children are under the authority and protection of their parents or legal guardian outside of extreme circumstances.
- Children should not be removed from or kept from their parents except under court order (extreme circumstances).
- The Child deserve to have their voices heard, and their votes counted through proxy-parental-voting rights, which would entitle parents to be the voting voice for their children.

- Children have the right to Life, Liberty, and the Pursuit of Happiness, just as any other American.
- Have the right to play, explore, learn, grow, be creative, and imaginative. I suggest we get out of the way of parents and allow them to nurture their children

rather than allow "the system" to crush them.

- WE have a duty to protect our children from sexual predators, abductors, and molesters. I believe WE need to recognize the problem, which is a high recidivism rate among sexual predators. Then take action and implement a strategy to remove the opportunity for sexual predators to strike again, and again, and again. More on this later.

- If 16 years old is closer to the maturity we expect to see in an adult community, and if our judicial system is inclined to charge minors as adults, it's time to review our nation's policy related to the age of accountability.
- If a child is charged as an adult, from that moment on the child-adult must be given the benefits and responsibilities of adulthood also (driving, military enlistment, drinking, smoking, decision making, voting, ability to enter into contracts, serve alcohol, etcetera).
- If a child serves in the military prior to 18 years of age, that child is now a legal adult, entitled to all benefits and obligations expected of an adult.

10.

CONSTITUTIONAL LAW/ LAW ENFORCEMENT PROTECTION ADVOCACY (CLLEPA)

- Protects and defends the Constitutional Rights that have been endowed to U.S. by Our Creator, and laid out plainly in our Constitution.

- It would the public's Police Agency emplaced to protect against corruption within all governing and Law Enforcement agencies, at any level inside, or outside, the government.

- Complete, transparent, interactive, public oversight and controls available around the clock.

- Legal representation provided free of charge

11.

CORRUPTION IN GOVERNMENT

- Because the politically elite have abused their seats of power, I suggest we mandate that all elected officials must be surveiled 24/7 using similar advanced surveillance tools that have been used on the unsuspecting public for decades to monitor our elected officials while in office, for security, transparency, and for the necessary protection of our freedom and privacy in OUR homes and lives. I know it may sound like I might be going too far with this, but hear me out, I believe our way of life necessitates it.

- I suggest we establish an official, public Internet location where factual evidence can be gathered on our public servants. A place where the words and promises made can be tracked and actual actions can be compared and analyzed. Allow all citizens full access to this site, and allow for conversation, debate, quotes, links, pictures, videos, and statements can be categorized, indexed, and readily accessed.

- Checklists can compiled and track whether individuals are keeping their word, being faithful representatives, or not...and if not they have a history that can be used for their rapid removal.

- Timeline incorporation helpful, and can serve as a historical database for our education outlet.
- Similar to Wikipedia, users can update site as needed.
- Much, if not most evidence will hopefully validate the politicians—allowing for a track record to be established, and allowing for easy access to understanding a politician's actual position, voting history, statements, alliances, etc. but, when corruption has been established, a complete investigation into all actions taken whilst in an official capacity must be undertaken.

- Removal of a corrupt public servant from their position of trust should be swift, and a thorough investigation into the purported actions/violations over the course of their incumbency would need to be performed. All policy changes instituted by such an incumbent would require overturning and reversing such changes, to include neutralizing their votes while in office, and performing the necessary recounts, etc.

- When an elected official has been released from duty, honorably, or otherwise, it should be standard operating procedure to perform follow-up investigations into the finances of these individuals, thereafter to ensure that corrupt elected officials haven't accepted post-office pay-offs for actions performed while in office on the behalf of influential entities pushing their own agendas.

12.

DNA

- Each individual has the right to his or her own personal DNA.

- Each individual has the right to not have be cloned or to have their fetal, or other DNA used outside of their express consent.

- Hospitals, blood donations, disallowed from collecting, personally profiling, and cataloging patient's DNA without consent. Care (and blood collection) must be provided for, regardless of refusal to consent.

13.

ELECTRO MAGNETIC PULSES (EMPs)

- We know that Iran, and others wish to attack using an EMP. We must deter those with known desires from ever attacking in such a manner.
- Establish a contingency plan immediately, in case of imminent attack prior to hardening of the system.
- Immediately take action to harden our delicate infrastructure and consider using Corps of Engineers to assist.
- Source, manufacture, and stockpile vulnerable electricity grid components within the U.S.A.
- Return to the practice of manufacturing of expensive, key components within the U.S.A.
- Create incentives at the Local and State levels to exceed minimum hardening (levels of protection) standards within their communities.
- Develop end incorporate shielding technology standards that mandate protections from EMPs on individual's vehicles, homes, electronics, and etc.
- Develop solid-state vehicular computer alternatives for the public that can be

swapped out in case of an EMP emergency.

- Remove FCC regulation that requires all harmful interference be allowed within an owner's electronics.

- Educate the public.

14.

ENERGY, OIL & OTHER

- Support utilizing Thorium in our reactors rather than Plutonium (no radioactive waste pollution to deal with). It is also a good compromise to nations that demand nuclear reactors for peaceful reasons.

- Support the effort to provide energy as a free resource if possible.

- I desire to implement many of Nicolai Tesla's discoveries today.

- Put a stop to purchasing our energy from our enemies.

- "Cap and trade" needs to be undone—and I support utilizing advances in cleaner burning coal alternatives rather than doing away with the industry altogether

- Support the utilization of our natural resources in a responsible manner

- Support joining efforts with our international neighbors, chiefly Mexico and Canada, in finding and tapping into all of our natural resources more efficiently, and creating "win-win", purchase and exchange agreements that promote better relations and prosperity.

- Support sharing advanced energy technologies with international community.

- Support actively finding and implementing cost-effective alternatives to oil, in a rapid manner.
- Such as hydrogen energy alternatives
- Energy from water is likely one of our best future energy sources. H2O—Hydrogen is explosive, and Oxygen is required for combustion, split the water molecule and you've got clean-burning energy, in abundance, with water as the "pollutant" or emission. Advances in understanding microwave technology have shown U.S. the way to split the water molecule efficiently. Now let's do something with it.

15.

ENVIRONMENTAL PROTECTION AGENCY (EPA) & CAP AND TRADE

- I recognize that the EPA is out of control.

- We need to decrease their power and decrease their control (strip them of it, and likely disband this establishment altogether, keeping what is of benefit to Americans, and discarding what is not). Pick it, wash it, cut it, pare it, and discard the waste (fraud, abuse, and money).

- A thorough audit/assessment is needed to determine the scope of this problem
- Immediately reign in their authority and negative influence on society
- Review and dismantle their regulations imposed on society. Congress can impose the various laws that are required to benefit We, The People.

- Focus on increasing freedom in America, and removing the fetters that bind our farmers and ranchers from providing nutritious food, worldwide.

16.

FAMILIES

- Healthy, thriving Families are important to the success of America, and therefore, the world.

- Parents have a responsibility for, and authority over their children until the legal age of accountability.
- Parents have the right to rear their children and to educate them in their homes, or at any other location of their choosing, without harassment or penalty. Rather, this practice needs to be encouraged. Especially during times such as these. Look at the problems happening within our education system. Is there any wonder that it is failing U.S.?

- Parents have the Legal right to guide their children's religious beliefs, however they deem appropriate, morally, without government intrusion, nor penalty.

- Parents have the right, and moral obligation, to direct their children's medical care and to not have their children taken from their custody, even if/when physicians disagree with that parent's decision.
- Parents have the right to Choose, Time, and Refuse immunizations for themselves, and for their children, against

medical advice (AMA) and without fear of retribution (without a court order).

- Parents have the right to refuse social services and any intrusion they may pose to their homes and lives, without retribution or penalty.

- I believe the family unit is being underrepresented, and underserved. I believe it is time for the voices of our children to be heard at the ballot box. I believe parents should be entitled to vote for their children (in proxy). I would like to see this possibility opened up for discussion and hopefully Amendment.

- Provide tools for parents that actually help them regulate what viewing material is welcomed into their homes. *Develop software which allows the community to apply their own rating systems, with specialized editing tools and filters to allow users to choose what type of language, images, sexuality, etcetera, that are viewed from their TV, phones, and other devices that access public space.

17.

FARMERS & FARMING / RANCHERS & RANCHING

- Assess ALL current major issues that these communities are currently facing and seek to decrease and/or remove infringing regulations placed upon them.
- Seek to stimulate this industry into higher production and prosperity for both those doing the work, and those receiving the benefit of their work.

- Place Farmers' and humanity's welfare above that of general land, lakes, and animals.
- Place the persons' welfare before that of the bug or road when deciding policies that affect our food production and producers. No perceived endangered/threatened insect should be cause enough to force Farmers to change their operations and/or receive punitive costs associated with.

- Support and defend the rights of Farmers/Ranchers and All Americans to be productive, prosperous, and to pursue their own form of happiness, and subsequently, to work out their own salvation.
- I move to undo much of the harm that has been worked upon this industry over the

past several decades (at least) due directly to government overreach.

- Remove barriers to entry into farming and ranching, increase support for entry into this field, and encourage Americans to enter the agricultural field by providing land grants and professional expertise and counseling. There will be a lot more hungry people Inside and Outside Our country, and Our Shores before long.

18.

FEDERAL GOVERNMENT MONEY MANAGEMENT

- Assess Current Situation
- Stop All Payments to Our Enemies. (We need to triage Our Alliance). Assess, and Consider Stopping Most International Payments for Unknown, or Wasteful Reasons. Allow for Complete Public Oversight, and Voting on charitable donations to governments, and etc.

- Implement Standing Policy to Identify and Reduce Waste, Fraud and Abuse.
- Increased Public Oversight of Itemized Spending, including the ability to view, question, document, and correct wasteful spending.
- Removal of government employees who entertain Waste Fraud and Abuse.
- Government, Political employees will purchase their own meals, and bottled water, and refreshments, etc. Didn't congress spend a million on bottled water one year?
- Reduced pay for elected positions, Especially Higher Offices.

- Public encouraged to help direct government to lower-cost alternatives to products and services.
- Government purchasing not limited to their normal vendors. No vendors

eliminated from vendor pool. Best Bargain Wins the Bid.

- Governments exit from the "Drug War" should reduce Wasteful, Fraudulent, and Abusive Spending.

- Establishment of Perpetualized funding and Outleting, as a moral, cost effective alternative to the present taxpayer-financed, never-ending drain on taxpayer resources, loss of purpose, and loss of public controls.
- Many government agencies can be reduced to each constituents' best parts and then merged together to form something better, and freer, networked, and finally, cut loose from federal ties, to be handed over to We, The People.

- Returning federal lands to the states in which they reside.
- Utilize existing property infrastructure, or release it to the states where they reside.
- Retrofit federal property to help house the homeless.

19.

FEDERAL RESERVE / GOLD STANDARD / GOLD RESERVES

- Temporarily the Federal Reserve will be directed to pay all taxes (everyone pays a fair share through inflation, there will be no need to individually file).

- The Federal Reserve director will be replaced with an honest individual (who We elect) to do the will of The People.

- Inspector General will perform audit of gold reserves, and provide We, The People with the final report, and quarterly reports thereafter.
- Gold, sitting in the reserves belongs to The American People, particularly because it was forcibly taken, exchanged for about half of what it was worth (in fiat currency) then melted down, and stored in various locations around the U.S. (We hope).

- Dollars will be compared with our gold reserves, and a quarterly dollar for gold/silver/copper/other commodity, rate will be established. Each time a dollar is exchanged (cashed) for a government held commodity, that dollar would be destroyed. Each dollar can be individually tracked through its serial number for validity.

- After the Jubilee, the Federal Reserve will be dismantled and done away with. The strength of the dollar will be restored to The People.

- After the Jubilee, a flat tax rate (FTR) for All Americans will be voted on and made law.

20.

FOOD AND DRUG ADMINISTRATION (FDA)

- Assess the usefulness of this tax-funded establishment.
- Provide for a thorough, transparent, publically guided audit.
- Decrease their power and negative influence on society.
- Review all regulations now in place keeping only those deemed constitutional, and worthy of passing laws for.
- Recognize that Americans have the right to ingest any substance they so choose. Therefore, the FDA is not [should not be] constitutionally able to force their regulations upon society, but rather be an entity that enlightens.

21.

FOREIGN FINANCIAL AID / FOREIGN FUNDING

- Recognize that we, as a nation, are in debt, and in fact can use some debt relief ourselves.

- We need to put an end to the practice of assisting our enemies with financial aid.
- Before any giving such aid, I believe We, The People, have the right to vote on who gets charitable contributions in Our name.

- When in office I'll put the brakes on all foreign aid payments until all have been reviewed and justified. No funding will go to support our enemies.

- Transparency is mandatory, and public oversight and controls are critical.

22.

FREEDOM OF SPEECH / PRESS

- Shall not be infringed, restricted, nor controlled.

- Whitehouse press briefings must be open to all reporters, not just the reporters the current president favors.

- Constitutional oversight board to be created to investigate abuses and to defend the rights of its citizens, whistleblowers, and the press. This board is to be controlled by We, The People, possibly working alongside the Inspector General, and would be cost-free to users.

23.

FRIEND? OR FOE?

- Allow for all nations of the world to formally announce their alliance or not, publicly, officially, for a set period of time. Countries would understand that by not voicing their position they would be counted as an enemy to our state.

- Assess the outcome and form official alliances

- We would then hold a special election to vote on our proposed alliances, and then, formulate, and extend friendship to those within our New-Alliance.

- Building upon each allies' strengths, we will formulate our strategy

- Strengthen that alliance.

- Rescue Righteous Refugees.

- Contain and/or destroy threats posed by enemies and to the alliance.

- Hold An Annual International Celebration with massive fireworks displays and much more.

HEALTHCARE

- Streamline the costs for care.

- Minimum standards need to be established in these areas:
  - Patient nurse ratio
  - Doctor patient ratio
  - Standardized minimums established in regards to the actual face-to-face time doctors spend with their inpatient patients.
  - Patient and provider bill of rights
  - Video-recordings of all surgeries performed provided to patient.
  - Around the clock video-recordings maintained and provided for all in-patient patients (opt-out available).
  - Patient healthcare records to be provided immediately after service has been rendered, and protected from government intrusion, to include those entities that regularly enter the healthcare setting and randomly review patient-records unbeknownst to the actual patient. Patients have the right to privacy, period.

- Severe penalties mandated for failing to preserve patient privacy.
- Patients to be alerted whenever their medical records have been accessed, with reason for being accessed provided.
- Require hand-washing of all who enter a healthcare premises
- Increase awareness of the benefits of hand washing broadcasted.
- RFID (or other technology) pass-card/beeper check-in for patients, that eliminates the requirement to physically check-in at the doctor's office, pharmacy, and emergency room, etc. This pass-card/beeper would alert the patient that the provider is about ready to see them.
- RFID tracking of patients, visitors, nurses, doctors, and other employees within the hospital setting that would track locations, assist in documentation process, and assist in reduction of paperwork requirements.
- Contingency plans established for Ebola-like outbreaks

- Discounted rates must be charged to the recipient of care, if non-doctors, in their stead, render that care. And this, so long as the non-doctors are compensated at lower rates by the facility that employs them (if that's the case). The charge to the paying customer must be relative to what it costs to pay their caregivers.

25.

HEINOUS CRIMES & CRIMINALS

I support severe penalties, up to and including permanent incarceration, labor, and/or death penalty, for individuals found guilty of any of the following crimes (in no particular order):

- Rape
- Murder
- Enslavement
- Sex enslavement
- Kidnapping by stranger
- Treason
- Conspiracy to commit heinous crimes
- Pedophilia
- Torture
- And other similarly heinous crimes against humanity

26.

HIGHER EDUCATION

- Internet version available free of charge to all who have met basic prerequisites.

- Any student can undertake any subject course at any time, once enrolled.
- Additionally, any student can also change their course of study at any time of their choosing, and begin from where they now stand, without penalty.
- In fact, a person could spend their lifetime in study if they choose to do so.

- Existing private establishments of higher learning can compete with free.

- Teachers will be openly graded by their students and by their peers, and their track records will be clearly established, and made available to all who might want to learn from them.

27.

HOMEOWNER'S ASSOCIATIONS

- Homeowners have a right to opt-out, individually.

- Support increased constitutional defenses and protections for homeowners.

- Support the view that a homeowner is the ruler of their castle. Sovereign.

- Simplify process for homeowners association's (HOA) removal, when communities desire this action.

- American flags are protected, and all individuals have the right to fly their flag, so long as proper care and respect is given and all federal regulations are followed.

- Homeowner's Constitutional rights trump any HOA agreement.

- HOA dues rates, if any, are to be locked in for duration, and to be maintained at that rate until that rate be voted into change. All new residents would enjoy the same locked in rate as the original homeowner.

28.

HOME-SCHOOLING / PARENT TEACHERS

- I'm in strong support for increased homeschooling in American homes.

- Parents and legal guardians have the Moral right to teach their children within the confines of their home, or any other location of their choosing.

- Home-schooling is safer, there are no bullies to worry about, no bullets to worry about, no unwanted propagandist teachings to worry about, no parent-teacher conferences to work out and stress out about, less spending on child care, and there are significantly fewer sex-offender risks, and even less risk of having your child ripped out of their chair by a high school cop.

- We have this great blessing of technology in our homes that can allow everyone to get an education within the walls of their own private homes.
- Provide open educational access to all the tools and materials needed to support parents who choose this path.
- Provide the required Internet access for family educators.

- Co-ops encouraged.

- At-work, private, employer-based, educational co-ops, for employees' children, promoted as an option/incentive for parents who can't leave their children at home and choose to "opt-out" of the public education system, but are unable to educate at home, or choose not to.

- Financial incentives for home schooling, workplace schooling, and co-op schooling.

- Athletics opportunities and pathways for home-schooled children established and expanded.

- Allows for increased independence and ability to provide for ones' self, both on and off grid.

29.

HOSPITAL RIGHTS & RESPONSIBILITIES

Right to Self Determination:

- Right to determine what procedures are off-limits within their establishment.

- Responsibility to verify the credentials and abilities of all professionals and assistive personnel.

Financial Responsibilities:

- Responsibility to assist in providing an estimate of costs prior to charging customers (similar to what a mechanic does). Provide documented costs and options associated with services, and enter into contract with each patient.

- Responsibility to track all patient charges throughout their stay or visit (on a per/minute basis), and include all equipment used/charged

- Patients need not be charged for the mistakes of their provider. For example, if a nurse places an indwelling catheter improperly, forcing the nurse to obtain and place a new catheter, the hospital must absorb that cost, not the patient. And, when a patient gets sick or injured due to the establishment's negligence, the patient must be compensated for their pain, suffering, and losses related to this negligence/error. It must be built in and established nationally, for rapid compensation.

Security and Firearms:

- Provide security, and provide secure on-site lockers for patients, visitors, and employee weapon stowage.

- Responsibility to secure patient records and documents from all entities that are not directly involved with providing that patient's care. This includes the government and its agents, without a court order.

- Right to refuse to cooperate with JACHO/TJC, as well as other government and nongovernment oversight entities, except when required by a court order. Patients and their attorneys will be responsible for bringing cases to the court when providers are failing.

- Focus on increased privacy, cost reduction, and reduction in caregiver workload. Stop the dog and pony show. Wasteful quick preparation by hospitals and clinics does little to protect the patient.

Transparency, Sanitization, Patient Comfort:

- Mandatory public reporting and recording of all accidental deaths / sentinel events on hospital/clinics' websites, over the life of the business, and made readily available to all patrons of the facility, while at the facility.

- Responsibility to maintain or exceed the highest levels of healthy of sanitization.
- Responsibility to provide sanitary bathrooms that are equipped with barrier protections for the toilets, touchless entry and exits, soap, water, flushing, drying, and lighting.

- Provide in-patient patients the ability to self-regulate the temperature within their rooms within a safe range.

Cost Controls:

- Hospitals and providers must not be bound and limited to a single product supplier. We need to defend their right to choose their products and devices based upon cost and quality, and to not be limited to a single supplier (healthy market competition is good for U.S. all).

Provide Rest/Sleep Areas:

- Rest/sleep areas required within hospital setting for waiting patients in emergency department.

- Rest/sleep areas required for medical staff, and allowed to be accessed when relief is needed (remember patient safety is number one priority, safety is increased when staff is talented, rested and focused.

Many nurses and assistive personnel work 12 hour shifts, half of them work the night shift which takes a heavier toll on most individuals, extra rest would be beneficial in certain common scenarios).

- Mandatory, regular breaks, with penalties for not taking breaks, or for not ensuring breaks are being taken, for all healthcare caregivers. Some nurses and assistive personnel work will habitually go an entire work shift without ever taking the time to urinate, or drink water. This can't be safe, for anyone.

30.

HUMAN LIBERTIES (MANKINDS' LIBERTIES)

- Freedom to live one's life according to the dictates of one's conscience
- Right to be told the truth by the elected, both on, and off the record.
- Freedom to fail or succeed
- Freedom to not be forced to receive inoculations
- Right to be left alone
- Right to pay your fair tax once for your property, and then never have the government come asking for more.
- You have the right to not be forced to do something you object to doing. You therefore have the sovereign Right, as a human, to "opt-out" of any activity deemed immoral, or otherwise offensive to you, individual. For example, no person can be forced to perform or to assist with an abortion, or an execution, or even a homosexual union, even if it means upsetting the boss at work, and maybe an entire community.

HUMAN RIGHTS – ALL INCLUSIVE

- All people share the same God-given rights and protections and responsibilities *see U.S. Constitution and Bill of Rights.
- All people have the Responsibility to respect the rights of others to pursue their own form of happiness.
- All people enjoy the Right of Conscience *see First Amendment
- All people enjoy the Right to preach their gospel, and to be preached to by others *politically protected.

32.

ILLEGAL IMMIGRATION / IMMIGRANTS

- Today, We, The People accept responsibility for allowing the conditions that have invited millions of illegal immigrants to our country. Because of this I believe a temporary moratorium on penalizing these individuals needs be imposed. Thereby providing temporary permission for these individuals to remain in Our country, with the condition that they turn themselves in and begin the immigration triage process if they desire to stay.

- However all amnesty granted immigrants (prior illegal immigrant status) will be required to pay an additional 2% tax for life (or until the time the problem is resolved completely) to assist in the recoupment of costs associated with their unethical activity.

- We should attempt to assimilate all who we can, and deport, reject, or incarcerate (for criminal activity [if applicable]) those who we can't.
- Felons, outlaws, and individuals having violent histories to be charged, incarcerated, and processed according to our laws when captured.
- All illegal immigrants who are convicted of a crime must be placed into low-cost,

work-labor penitentiaries, until the costs associated with their specific activity has been recuperated.

- We cannot reward those who actively circumvent our immigration system. The practice of illegally entering Our country, in order to deliver a baby free of charge, only to be rewarded citizenship, is insane. And must be stopped.

- I suggest we establish a two-strikes law that when broken through future illegal immigration would result in three years work-labor, confinement, followed by deportation, and legal citizenship pathway education, as well as placement onto the U.S. no-fly, no-float list, Our no-entry list, and a 5 year wait prior to being considered for reentry, legally, into the U.S.A.

- All illegal immigrants and those granted amnesty or refugee status would need to be entered into the HIIDE system, a system that utilizes biometrics for identification, and have their DNA collected and entered into the national database for review of criminal activity.

- Illegal immigrants will incur a debt to the Nation and sign into a debt to society agreement, swear allegiance to the U.S. Constitution, pledge allegiance to Our Flag, agree to 240 total hours volunteer work at immigration, detention and refugee processing centers, and incur a lifetime additional flat tax rate of 2% atop their total annual wages/pensions for life or resolution. These monies collected through this process will be used to offset the costs related to the burden placed upon the American systems—chiefly healthcare, traffic, judicial, education, criminal activity, etc., etc., and those monies will then be distributed to the aforementioned systems accordingly.

33.

IMMIGRATION / CITIZENSHIP & NATURALIZATION

- Christian and Jewish refugees get priority immigration status.
- No countries' immigrants to receive monetary compensation for immigrating to the U.S. except for refugees.

- Require online Constitutional Continuing Education (CCEs) completion and proficiency, as the first step in Our immigration process, prior to spending any money, and require continuing education for the next five years, free of charge, prior to being granted voting rights.

- Have the costs associated with the various pathways through immigration, to citizenship clearly established for All People, documented, and have costs reduced over time as the process becomes more efficient.

- All amnesty granted immigrants (prior illegal immigrant status) will be required to pay a 2% tax penalty, for life, to assist in the recoupment of costs associated with their immigration pathway choice, and the expenses associated with it.

- Citizenship needs to be conditional until completion of five years of CCEs and ten years of law abidance has been established.

- Voting rights granted once five years of CCEs have been successfully completed, and provisional status of residency removed.

- The system to be perpetually funded by those who use it, be simple, be fully transparent in nature, and be federally regulated with powerful public oversight.

- Almost all people, everywhere, are welcome to immigrate, so long as they go through the front door. All line-cutters to go to the back of the line (this means if you enter our country illegally, and are captured, your process is delayed by three years, after restitution.
- Repeated line-cutters will be required to pay for the costs associated with their criminal activity. In most cases, this will likely mean indentured service (forced labor) at a standard wage rate, until all costs associated with their capture, incarceration, detention, legal, and transportation costs are recuperated.

Exceptions:

- No sex-offenders are eligible for citizenship. Any captured sex-offenders from anywhere, or anywhen, are to be tried and incarcerated. The high recidivism rate requires permanent removal from society.

- Murderers must pass extra scrutiny to include acceptance by a moral-board hearing. Ten years must have passed since last date of incarceration, prior to immigration.

- Felons must pass a felon's-review-board prior to beginning the immigration process (outside studying the Constitution). Five years must have elapsed since last incarceration date.

- Mandatory health-review related to infectious diseases performed upon arrival to a refugee welcome center, or Ellis Island.

- All new immigrants must submit fingerprints, DNA, and biometrics prior to permanent residency, and they must be entered into the national database, and checked against possible criminal activity, and maintained.

- Citizenship conditional upon law abidance for ten years.

34.

INCARCERATION & REHABILITATION

- Focus on rehabilitating our inmates rather than continuing down our current path.
- Provide pathways that assist individuals in shifting from a life of crime, to a life with purpose and meaning.

- Law enforcement officers would be encouraged to assist in building this system because of their unique career exposure and experience, as well as for the therapeutic value that would be a benefit to the individual officer and to society as a whole.

- Because crime will be reduced through elimination of substance-prohibition, many law enforcement officers will likely need to transition to new jobs. So, what we do is provide these officers with the training and education necessary to work within this new rehabilitation/charitable welfare system, and follow the same pattern with other transitioning systems.

35.

INCREASED WAGES, WAGES IN GENERAL

- Reduced taxation and fewer people in the workforce should allow for increased wages for those who remain in it.

- Many families will take advantage of homeschooling, which allows for increased freedom, time, and money.

- Minimum wages must be done away with, or applied equally, across the spectrum. For example, just because a person gets tips shouldn't negate the business-owner's responsibility to pay their employee federally mandated minimum wage.

- Women get equal pay for identical jobs (in government).

- Soldier wages increased to match the national average, plus 25% for those in combat action (across the board) E-1 and up.

- Politician wages decreasing to match the national average, to include the president's wage. No federal politician will be paid more than the national average household income.

36.

INDIVIDUAL RIGHTS

- Please read the U.S. Constitution, all the Amendments, and the Declaration of Independence.
- I support strict adherence to and respect of the Bill of Rights.

- I view the Individual as Sovereign. So long as the individual is not harassing others or breaking our laws, they have the right to be left alone.

- The Individual DOES have a Right to their Property. I will do all I can to defend, protect, advance, and ensure that our individual civil rights are protected, defended, and advanced.

- Local, state, and federal agencies directed not to infringe upon the sovereignty of the American citizen (err on the side of Civil Rights).

- I suggest the establishment of a Constitutional Law/Law Enforcement Protection Advocacy (CLLEPA). We, The People, would directly overwatch this Advocacy. Boards, courts, and hearings would be established to challenge the constitutionality of actions taken by purported violators.

- CLLEPA exists to ensure law enforcement, government agencies, or international treaties do not infringe upon the rights of We, The People, specifically. They would exist for The People, by The People (versus for the people by the government).

37.

INTERNET

- Right to Free Speech
- Right to Freedom From Intrusion
- Right to Exist Without Internet Access

- Users have a right to remain anonymous, without harassment/punishment
- Freedom from government snooping/tracking/recording.

- Those who use it will regulate the Internet. The federal government has the responsibility to assist in restoring it to the bastion of Freedom it once was believed it could be, or was.

- Net Neutrality needs to be undone.

- Powers given over to The People.

- Even though I believe in freedom from snooping, I believe public welfare trumps limited snooping within certain defined purposes and limitations. I believe We should utilize the full strength of our technological capacity to monitoring those who are convicted felons.

- Outsize the aforementioned activities, the federal government needs to take a "hands-off" approach to the Internet whilst assisting in the defense of existing and future infrastructure, and allowing for military offensive/defensive applications, while acting within our Constitutional framework.

- Since We, The People enjoy the right to freedom from unwarranted searches and seizures, among many other rights, No charges may be brought against any individual based solely upon Internet data, except within the aforementioned cases and circumstances.

- Freedom from warrantless online data being used against an individual except in cases of Rape, Murder, Torture, Kidnapping, Slavery, Treason, Actual Terrorism, Sex Trafficking, and other heinous crimes of a serious nature.

- A caveat, No images, videos, nor other recordings obtained through lawful government surveillance can be allowed to be maintained, cataloged, viewed, nor released, etcetera, by government officials. All explicit material, except when part of a serious investigation, must be kept private (anonymized) and destroyed when discovered.

38.

IRAN

- The Iranian government has repeatedly, openly declared war on U.S. and our Allies.

- As an enemy, at war with U.S., this threat must be taken seriously, with a decisive strategy implemented if peace proves impossible.

39.

ISRAEL

- I am a friend to Israel.
- I stand with Israel.

- I seek the total restoration of Our Alliance and Friendship with Israel.

- I seek to assist in the defense and support of Israel, and in the rescue of all Christian refugees everywhere.

40.

JUBILEE & DEBT ~ AMERICAN NATIONAL & FOREIGN DEBT

- We cannot leave this massive debt to our children and grandchildren.
- I suggest taking a lesson from history and implementing a Jubilee that creates massive economic relief.
- TOTAL economic reset and relief (debt emancipation).

- Offer Jubilee to the international community. Those who participate will receive our friendship and debt forgiveness, and those who don't will be repaid in U.S. dollars.

- The day after the Jubilee, business begins anew, with the next Jubilee in fifty years.

Through This Action, We Will:

- Preserve our dollar
- Preserve/restore capitalism
- Return to gold standard
- Phase out the Federal Reserve
- Provide massive economic stimulus and widespread debt relief.
- Possibly avoid WWIII

41.

JUSTICE SYSTEM CORRUPTION

- I support expiring most laws, and attaching expiration dates to all new laws.
- I desire simplification of our laws
- I believe that The Constitution must be the defining legal standard that rules within the courts.
- I support the creation of a Constitutional Law/Law Enforcement Protection Advocacy (CLLEPA) that is available to and for All People, free of charge, whose rights have been violated.
- I would like to see justice officials, law enforcement officers, lawyers, and the courts openly graded by all who use The System.
- I want to place recording cameras in all courtrooms, for all proceedings, freely viewable by the public, and archived, etc.
- I seek the elimination of substance laws that put people in jail for use, sale, transportation, and consumption of any drug or substance. I believe it's time to end Prohibition for good.

- I support a Constitutional Amendment to officially bring an End to Prohibition, for good, again.

- Release, rehabilitate, educate, release, and possibly compensate those with current, or past drug offenses of record.

- Disallow "Prison-only" in-house justice hearings for offenses performed while incarcerated. I support total transparency of the legal system. I support Video-recording it completely, and provide for public viewing and oversight, with a clearly established, just, appeals process.

42.

LAW ENFORCEMENT

- Must be trained in the recognition of, limitations of, defense of, and protections afforded to each citizen, U.S. Constitution and the Bill of Rights.

- Officers need to be personally responsible for their actions, and therefore open to lawsuit by any citizen who believes their rights have been violated.

- Support increased public oversight

- No officer is above the law. Officers must be held to the same standard as those they police.

- Necessary to remove the incentives to violate Civil Rights. Drug-bust booty, seized items, vehicles, cash, fines, and other funding arising outside of normal government channels to be outlawed.

- Support the requirement that law enforcement agents reside within the communities they serve.

- Officers need to be psychologically, and peer reviewed regularly, with their arrest/detention records audited regularly, with public oversight, and openly graded.

- Support term limits for stagnant officers.

- Responsibility to be professional, helpful, compassionate, and merciful.

- Responsibility to provide actual identification to the civilians they serve.

- Under my guidance, law enforcement would not be allowed access to private property (including driveways, porches, walkways, lawns, doors) while on duty, without invitation or warrant, except when emergencies arise or while investigating a relevant crime.

- If you are an officer reading this, know that these changes will result in a simplified, more rewarding career path that has significantly less danger (for many).

43.

LOCAL RIGHTS

- Localities enjoy their own form of sovereignty too. This sovereignty is not to be suppressed from above; any suppression reported/discovered will receive federal constitutional relief.

- Individualism is necessary and expected

- State and federal government not to over-police, nor over regulate
- Implement a hands-off approach
- Private property respected and protected

44.

MANDATORY REQUIREMENT FOR HEALTH INSURANCE (OBAMACARE)

- Provide for an immediate opt-out option for everyone.

- Remove fines and return all fine money received thus far.

- Consider amending the constitution to keep this from happening again
- Immediately offer We, The People the option to opt-out of mandatory healthcare.

- Disengage from federal healthcare oversight—return oversight to We, The People.

45.

MARRIAGE ~ STRAIGHT, PLURAL, GAY & OTHER

- Government needs to take a non-intrusive; "hands-off" approach to all things related to marriage, and the family. The government can document and track marriages, but will not be the officiating officer any longer, and civil unions can be performed in front of a Notary Public, that is, so long as there is a willing notary to provide this service.

- You have the right to decide for yourself who you marry, and can do so according to the dictates of your own conscience.

- Marriage is a religious freedom that needs no limits put on it by the federal government.

- The government needs to stay out of the bedroom. We don't need the government making laws related to our spiritual beliefs.

- All marriages allowed between consenting adults. Including plural unions of legally consenting adults.

- Government has no right to regulate this religious and personal decision.

- Each individual has the right to believe whatever he or she chooses to. They can like, or dislike, agree or disagree, that's okay. What's not okay is discriminating and treating anyone less than human, for any reason.

- Human rights/constitutional rights trump all. If we adhere to basic respects for the individual, then everything will fall into place.

- Don't judge. Be kind and respectful. It's okay to speak, and share, but we must respect the rights and boundaries of each other, and respect the Christian foundation our Republic is based upon.

46.

MEDICARE

- Medicare needs to be provided for all those who are presently using the system, but it needs to be phased out.

- We need to recognize and take THE MORAL responsibility for the problem our governing body has created for our aging and disabled community—and provide for their relief.

- Creation of a better system, based upon best evidence based practices and upon our lessons learned from our past failures.

47.

MILITARY

- The Armed Forces, and its members would be the first bill We, The People pay, under my presidency, and thereafter.

- I support a substantial increase in pay for members in the Armed Forces (streamlined pay that matches what the Average American Annual Individual Income [AAAII] is regardless of rank), and an even higher increase in pay for those who see combat (outside the wire).

- Establishment of a pension system for AFMs that pays each and every member, based upon total time served, rank attained, duties performed, citations achieved, overall achievement, combat tours, and injuries sustained. With this system, all members would be more appropriately thanked and supported by U.S. for their sacrifice and service.

- Each and every Armed Forces Member (AFM) has the right and responsibility to defend themselves and each other, on and off post. Second Amendment rights for our AFMs must be respected.

- AFMs need to defend their own installations. Handing this off to private security is a bad idea, in my estimation.

Return to the practice of having our military police, police military installations.

- I support selection of, cultivation of, and retention of the best individuals, for the strongest military offense/defense possible, period.

- I support a much higher standard of selection criteria for our future enlistees and officer candidates.

- I support treating our Armed Forces Members like the athletes they are, and provide them with that sort of fitness training, standard, nutrition, and pro-trainer support all the way through it.

- I support alternate service options availability for those who can't meet the entrance standards but desire to serve in and with, the Armed Forces.

- Since all types of people, and sexualities are allowed, private housing is required for all who receive the benefit of government housing, on, or off post.

48.

MOTHERS & CHILD REARING

- Recognize the major contribution to society our mothers provide

- Financially assist those families who decide to educate their children at home, and are successful at doing so

- Support their decision

- Have any government funding that normally follows a child, follow the child even when they are being educated in their homes, by their mothers, etc.

49.

NASA, DARPA, SKUNKWORKS, AREA 51

- Unite efforts of all government funded technology entities.

- Merge these high-tech space, air, land and sea bodies in such a way as to decrease expenditure, decrease redundancy, increase information and expertise exchange, and positive outcomes.

- Encourage sharing of technological gains within national community and provide for open-access forums for sharing of this information in the spirit of benefiting the general welfare of We, The People.

- Advance hydrogen technology and application while seeking alternative forms of energy and transportation that reduce environmental and financial waste, redundancy, and increases overall freedom for All Americans.

- Incorporate advances in technology to our sea, air, land and space travel options.
- Advance personal air travel capabilities.
- Incorporate Nicolai Tesla's technology into society's infrastructure.
- Advance secure communication technology.
- Advance efficiency in travel, period.

50.

NEW WORLD ORDER

- All governments enjoy sovereignty, recognize that the New World Order (NWO) is a form of subversion of The People's freedom, and is birthed from corruption and therefore must be avoided.

- No order established that follows the framework of any existing official policy now in existence. Corruption necessitates this restriction.

- Only new international order that can be established would be one that is agreed to by We, The People, through Constitutional amendment, and truthful, transparent open debate. For now, and always, The U.S. Constitution and The Declaration of Independence stand in full effect.

51.

PATIENT RIGHTS & RESPONSIBILITIES

Freedom of Choice:

- You have the right to refuse treatment of any type.

- You have the right to refuse inoculations, and to not be discriminated against, nor judged a lesser citizen for your decision (right to healthcare privacy mandates this is the right approach,). [once a citizen]

Right to Competent Care:

- You have the right to receive competent care.
- You have the right to a second opinion, and when two out of the three second opinions conflicts with the one, the patient has the right to a full refund from the odd doctor out.

- You, as a paying customer (patient) have the right to a certain minimum amount of face-to-face time with your physician and nursing staff (and have the option to be charged at a per minute rate, versus per stay/visit rate, or any combination of the two).
- You have the right to have your assigned nursing staff and assistive personnel, not so overworked that subpar (increasingly

error prone, often painful, and unnecessary) care is rendered.

Right to Be Respected and Represented:

- You have the right to be accompanied 100% of the time by a chosen individual—to include within the surgical setting.
- You maintain the right to be respected, including while "asleep," under general-anesthesia.
- No patient should be ogled, made the butt of a joke, nor mistreated while undergoing treatment.

Right to a Fair Estimate of Costs:

- You have the right to know the costs associated with your care plan, prior to receiving treatment, and have the right to a fair estimate of the costs prior to any receiving any charges—this would similar to what all legitimate mechanics provide for their automotive patrons.
- You have the right to receive a full disclosure of your treatment options versus the common practice of blindly accepting the bill at the end of your servicing, allowing you to choose between the various products and services you wish to receive, and therefore to pay for.

- You have the right to pay lower costs if serviced by lower paid, or volunteer staff (nurse practitioners, physician assistants, students, etc.).

- You have the right to a complete statement of fees, real-time, and also upon completion of services rendered, and you have the right to dispute those fees when necessary, and you have the responsibility to pay for legitimate services and/or products received.
- You have the right to choose to pay cash for your treatment rather than use an insurance company, and therefore have the right to refuse to carry healthcare insurance altogether, without government penalty. * an escape route for those of U.S. who would like to choose the "Cash Option", over otherwise mandatory health care insurance coverage will be enacted, immediately.

Right to Privacy:

- You have the right to privacy, even privacy from your insurance company.
- Having the right to privacy (outside the service and government setting) no employer has the right to mandate you to disclose your immunization history for purpose of employment, including amongst healthcare workers / professionals.
- The patient has the right to not be questioned about their firearms preferences and / or ownership. No firearms related documentation to be included within the patient record. Any existing references to the aforementioned must be purged/stricken from the record.

Right to Complete Access to Your Healthcare Record:

- You have the right to complete access to your healthcare record; to include doctor's notes, psych notes, recommendations, etc. Information that relates to you, as the patient, is not to be kept from you. If personnel places notations in your file, which are normally kept from patients, but is directly related to you, you have the right to see what is being said about you, and receive a copy of it. (No behind-the-scenes documentation, related to you, can be made off-limits to you, the customer).

- The patient has the right to have their treatments, advice, and surgeries video-recorded, and to receive immediate electronic access to it, indefinitely, free of charge.

- You have the right to have your care documented via paper-only means, and to receive the original copy of your documentation upon discharge or completion of treatment / appointment, etc.

- The facility/provider must obtain permission to maintain your documentation in their filing system, and/or on their servers.

- You have the right to have your records free from search by ANY governing body, including The Joint Commission (TJC) and any other entities out there, for any purpose (without express written permission).
- When and if your records have been accessed, by any individual, or entity, you, the client, have the right to be promptly notified of all interested parties, with reasons stated validating the who, what, when, and why they accessed your private information.
- Hospitals/facilities/providers must bear the burden of legal costs (for their patrons) related to privacy violations.

52.

PATRIOT ACT

- Dismantle it, cancel it, repeal it, veto it, and put an end to it, as soon as possible.

- Restore all lost freedoms to We, The People.

- Provide a comprehensive damage assessment to U.S.

- Provide total transparency and public oversight throughout the triage process.

53.

PERPETUAL EDUCATION

Internet-Based International Perpetual Education:

- Establishment of a New, Free, education system that is self-sustaining (post initial cash investment/infusion).

- Streamlined system that acts to assist the student with Their goals. Provides follow-up assistance, and coordination of Internet-based home-schooling resources.

- Reduce wasted spending on outdated models, and textbooks by shifting to open source electronic media. No physical textbooks required.

- Reduce costs and create a networked system of education pathways that can be self-propagating, from the input of individual users, parents, educators, experts, and etcetera.

- Increased service and income opportunities available to community volunteers, and "retired" or ageing, educators.

- Online resources available worldwide to the global community, free of charge, and the international community is encouraged to participate and assist in the creation of, and maintenance of, their own educational material, and collaborate with educators and students globally, etcetera.

- By creating this new system we will lower the tax burden and severely reduce waste, fraud, and abuse, along with severely reducing future costs associated with this system.

- WE will open the door to the infinite educational pathways that exist, and continue to expand daily. And WE'll open this door to knowledge, and wisdom, and Truth, to All People everywhere, and to support the individual as he/she chooses the education model (pathway) that best suits their self, their children, and their family, based upon whatever their goals, talents, and interest take them.

PERSONALLY OWNED VEHICLES & TRAFFIC

- I believe we should consider the vehicle an individual commands as an extension of their own physical body, and therefore off limits to unwarranted searches and seizures, and assaults.

- A single, initial registration of privately owned vehicles is sufficient. It's time to do away with the unnecessary extra financial burden imposed by the taxes, fines, and fees our government places on U.S. The People.

- No passport ever required when travelling in personally owned vehicle for U.S. citizens in America.

- Last I checked, 50,000 – 80,000 deaths occur on Our highways annually. The number of injured, permanently, and otherwise is staggering. When we compare the tiny percentage of deaths by firearms due to misuse, that number is lower than 10,000 (there are approximately 10,000 deaths by falls each year too, by the way). Comparing the number of accidental deaths occurring because of doctor error is in the ballpark of 50,000 annually, with a staggeringly high number of people left misdiagnosed, undiagnosed, under treated, over treated, or injured (please research this deeper to get at the actual numbers if desired).

- It is obvious We, The People have been paying much too much attention to firearms safety when we should have been focusing on making our roads, vehicles, and doctors safer for everyone.

- To that end, I propose we shift away from the current vehicular, roadway, traffic, and enforcement systems we have become accustomed to, and instead create safer intersections, roadways, vehicles, commonsense rules, with a penalty system that is outside the legal system (mostly) and does not penalize with fines and fees, but rather with intelligent alternatives, such as temporary driving restrictions, retraining, education, proficiency, etc. Convert much of the Highway Patrol (CHP)with Safe Highway Patrol (SHP) to assist in this transition. Remaining CHPs would be for surgical law enforcement when needed on our public highways.

- Analyze traffic problems and determine ways to reduce highway deaths, increase freedom, deter traffic accidents, abolish traffic fines, protect commuters, reduce stoppages, increase traffic flow, save money, and ensure rights, lives, and property of travellers are protected, and respected.

- Additionally, all highways, intersections, and other government owned cameras used for public surveillance are to be made accessible to ALL citizens, free of charge, 24/7. This will save money and assist in the reduction of crime and hit and run incidents.

55.

PERSONAL PROPERTY RIGHTS & RESPONSIBILITIES

- We, The People have the right to not have our property forcibly taken from U.S. by our government, or any other entity.

- I propose we do away with the corrupt practice of duplicitous taxation on our property. What I mean is that your property can only be taxed once. Once it has been taxed, it remains free from further taxation, forever, even if it is resold. This would definitely include vehicles, land, and real estate.

- Private property is not to be mandatorily, regularly registered, unless done so voluntarily, without fines, fees, nor penalties (this would indeed apply to firearms registration too).

- Firearms are not to be registered (simply) due to Our need to protect Our Second Amendment rights (as well as) each citizen's right to privacy and general protections from firearms seizures from corrupt and compromisable agents, databases, agencies, governments, and individuals (now and in the future [history has proven]).

- I will put a stop our government's habit of seizing private property (taking what's not theirs) and we will stop them from directly profiting from seizures when they are truly justified. This is a source of corruption and has become a problem on both the local and federal levels.

- Once property has be purchased, paid for, and possibly taxed, that object HAS BEEN TAXED and can no longer be taxed again, nor taken from its owner without a court order.
- This policy will require that property can only be taxed one time, regardless if a business is reselling it for a second or third time.
- Resold property is exempt from further taxation, even if it is sold for a profit at a later time.

- Regular cyclical registration of property is not required to own or operate any object, vehicle, nor property. The right to privacy must be maintained and reestablished.

- The individual owner of property has the responsibility to protect it from theft and misuse.

- Government no longer able to impose financial penalties upon individuals and businesses, without a court order.

- Government to respect the property and monies of We, The People. No seizures without court orders.
- Government not to benefit from cash / property seizures, including tax penalties and interest charges. All such seizures required to be distributed amongst the perpetually funded establishments across America. All such seizures to be made public and histories maintained.
- Property seizures cannot benefit the entity that seized it.
- Your cash cannot be seized by law enforcement solely based upon amount nor suspicion.
- Traffic violation no longer able to result in financial penalties / property seizures.

- Property to be respected and viewed as an extension of its owner.
- Property is related to our constitutionally protected pursuit of happiness. All such offenses against this right are to result in severe penalties imposed upon the abuser or entity.

- Imminent Domain powers severely reduced and compensation (when enforced) must be double the appraised value.

56.
PHYSICIAN RIGHTS & RESPONSIBILITIES

Freedom of Conscience:

- Right to self-directed, competitive pay
- Right to treat their families and friends without fear of reprisal.
- Right and responsibility to work within a safe environment (under normal conditions).
- Responsibility to act in patients' best interest by providing advocacy in the form of cost saving approaches and financial fairness.
- Right to choose, and to work with competent, fielded, licensed medical staff and right to choose their clientele (except under emergent conditions).
- Right to prescribe within the dictates of their conscience, their scope, and with agreement/understanding of their client.
- Freedom from government harassment, unnecessary oversight, complications, and freedom from filing fees for that oversight

Billing:

- Responsibility to spend standardized minimum mandatory time with patients, and to document actual time spent in research for and time spent physically with, and have a per minute rate established for clientele who choose that option for their billing (especially useful for patients who feel they are underserved by their physicians).

- Responsibility to provide a care-plan and financial disclosure to patients and their representatives, including the costs associated with their proposed care plan, prior to accruing charges for services, except in emergencies, in which cases the process will begin as soon as feasible.

Right to Teach Apprentices and to Bestow Medical Degrees:

- Right to provide certified, individualized accredited apprenticeships that result in medical degrees, within their scope of practice and level of proficiency.

57.

PLAN FOR SERVICE-MEMBERS / DEPLOYMENTS / NATIONAL DEFENSE

- Place the value of our service member's lives (and their families) above that of our equipment.

- Immediately work towards bringing most of our deployed service-members home.

- Retool, reset, recuperate, and recover before any further deployments.
- Plan for strategy against future attacks upon our nation and our allies.

- Defend our borders
- Provide mandatory training for constitutional protections
- Implement HIDE system for identification of all peoples residing in our country without proper documentation and authority. Begin processing those who meet this criterion.
- Recognize and reduce wasteful spending
- Revitalize our relations with our allies
- Retire / repurpose service members who do not meet the high standard required, provide prorated pensions.

- Officers need to go through Basic Training, Graduate from West Point (etc.) or be selected from Enlisted ranks prior to being given authority to Lead within the Combat Arms.

- Pay scale to be standardized for enlisted and commissioned (same pay scale).
- Pay to be increased for those who see combat action, and for those in combat arms and other highly toxic roles.
- Retention incentives for strength, fitness, experience, performance, intelligence, and needs of the military, regardless of prior retention incentives.

- Incorporate study of the U.S. Constitution, Declaration of Independence, and U.S. and world History within the Armed Forces.
- Require daily Pledging Allegiance to The Flag of The United States Of America. (All government jobs will now require this).

58.

PREGNANCY ASSISTANCE / RIGHT TO LIFE

- Since our U.S. Constitution requires to government to acknowledge, respect, and protect the individual's right to life, it must needs be that all (human) life must be protected (defended) and provided the optimal conditions for growth, and delivery, at the earliest possible time.

- This restoration of an age-old policy is about providing protections to new life and to the lives of expecting mothers—giving the developing fetus and the mother the best chance to grow healthy and strong (folic acid, drugs, testing, delivery, spiritual, social, emotional, physical, etc.).

- Creation of a Life Defense / Protection League that is perpetually funded and run by We, The People.

- Any woman needing assistance with meeting her pregnancy needs will be provided for At No Charge. However, assistance with assisting others with pregnancy needs would be requested (cost reduction).

- Massive online access to help, information, and resources
- Counseling made freely available
- Support network extended to the expectant mothers.

- Incentives provided for entrance into midwifery occupation

59.

PRISON SYSTEM

- Reform system into one that facilitates Rehabilitation and Reintegration

- Create and Support a framework that provides relocation services to inmates and provides all necessary counseling to those in need

- Education available and encouraged within the correctional system
- Release of simple drug offenders and review of all other drug related offenses. Expunge records where needed.

- Consolidate facilities, reduce costs

- Encourage inmate assisted animal rehabilitation programs and other proven (and otherwise) nonconventional methods to decrease pain, and facilitate recovery.

- 100% surveillance while incarcerated
- 100% surveillance for felons when released until proven track record established

- Sex-offenders don't get out to offend again

- Militarized (basic training style, with respect) –type control of inmates (no more using division among our people to control U.S. (fights, racial, gangs).

- Inmates earn their Rights back.

- Earn degree while incarcerated, fully transferrable outside system
- Provide assistance once returned to society.
- Create oversight panels for judgments passed on inmates for crimes committed while incarcerated

60.

PRIVACY / SNOOPING

- Americans have the right to be free from electronic intrusion / monitoring.

- We have the right to privacy of yourself, your phone, other electronics, health records, prescription history, immunization history, gun ownership, race, religion, sex, location, etc. if chosen.

- Even still, We, The People have the right to privacy, to include online, if so chosen. Anonymous usage allowed. If a user is online in an anonymous mode, they cannot access the personal information of any non-anonymous user. To access the personal information of another, the user must be willing to have their personal information logged and accessible to the person whose information has been accessed.

- Bank account information to be kept private, with severe penalties for privacy intrusion without a court order.

- All sexually explicit personal media discovered by government must be destroyed upon initial discovery, left unviewed, and if and when viewed, all who have viewed, and when and why they viewed it must be documented and made available to a federal oversight commission, to ensure the right to privacy is being maintained for We, The People.

- Unless criminal in nature, no explicit personal media may be cataloged, stored, nor released to the public. Rather, all such media must be electronically shredded when found. We have a right to be secure in our Homes, our Papers, and our Possessions.

61.

PROPANDA / PSYCHOLOGICAL OPERATIONS (PSY OPS) USAGE IN AMERICA

- Make illegal immediately
- Investigate and illuminate the public as to what has been used against them thus far, and the Who, What, When, Where, and Why's of the situation.
- Educate to keep from recurring.

62.

RACISM / HATE

- Racism can be found in every race. It's not limited to white versus black. Rather, it is an individual intolerance and hatred for another person, of another race, that is based upon twisted thoughts that resonate with evil.

- I believe we are all made in the image of our creator, God, our Heavenly Father. As such, I believe we must remember the example of our savior and his great Love for all, as was confirmed through his life, and his ultimate sacrifice. He did not judge a person by the color of their skin, but rather by the content of his character. We should do likewise.

- We too must Love one another and treat each other, as we would like to be treated. Simple golden rule stuff.

- All men and women are created equal.

- Pay and opportunities need to be open to all, and be based upon performance, ability, dependability, experience and honesty, among other important positive characteristics.

- Acts of intimidation and violence will not be tolerated.

- All businesses are welcome to be racist, and all potential patrons are welcome to not visit their business. Ultimately, the racist or bigoted business owner does US all a favor by openly telling us who they are (inside).

63.

RELIGION

- No law will be allowed to exist which attempts controls or influences or fines religious individuals, groups, establishments, or sects—except when such an entity actively seeks to infringe upon the Religious and Moral Rights of others—for example, seeking to destroy the Life, Liberty, Freedom, or Property of another.

- A Religion that seeks the destruction of another People and Their Beliefs cannot be granted Constitutional protections. Rather, Our Constitution stands resolutely against it. Therefore, in these situations, the individuals and leaders of this type of organization must be targeted, destroyed, captured, and/or tried for violating the rights of others (circumstances varying as they do). Their property seized, capitalized or destroyed, and then distributed among the perpetually funded public services.

- Religions (as well as All People) enjoy the Right to Free Speech and the Freedom of Thought.

- Religions are tax-exempt, and non-finable, without due process.

- Religions are free to teach, preach, and exonerate all to do well.

- Prayer is protected and no law can, should, nor shall, be made to control it. Rather, laws may need to be established to further protect it.

- Since America is founded upon Christianity, Christian prayer is protected and welcomed in our government establishments, schools, military, and legal systems, public and private.

- Sharia-law is practiced in many locations around this world, but, one place it is not recognized as valid, nor practiced, but rather outlawed, is in America, and needs to be, among our Alliance.

- All individuals are free to read religious texts openly, in public, without punishment, though no religion is free to broadcast their views forcefully into the common ear-waves (through loudspeaker, for example) when the majority present find it offensive.

64.

RIGHT TO BE

- We, The People, reserve Our Right to be Free and Independent. To become who, and what we choose.
- I'll be Me, You be You.
- We, The People, have a right to, and wish to Preserve our Freedom of Conscience.
- I Am a Man, and I choose to BE a Man. You BE You. I'm okay with that too.
- We don't collectively desire, nor tolerate assaults on anyone based on race, sexuality, religion, and/or belief systems. Rather, Americans are tolerant of the views of others, and each Citizen has the Right to be given the same respect.

65.

RIGHT TO INGEST – DRUGS, FOOD, POISON

- We don't always encourage the taking in of known toxic substances, but all Legal Adults have the right to ingest any substance of their choosing, and have the Right to be free from harassment (and to be free of criminal prosecution if they are not breaking any law whilst under the influence of it).

- This concept applies equally, to everyone, all the time. So, watch what you use, and how you use it. You will be held responsible for your actions.

- Almost all matter is legal for human consumption, though many might be considered hazardous to one's health. No law can be tolerated that punishes an Individual for what they choose to consume, or not to consume.

- Any outlawed substances would require Constitutional Amendment to be enforceable.

- Liberty should not be taken, and money not spent, nor seized from users of any substance. The Right to Pursue Happiness is defended in our Constitution.

- Prior drug convictions, fines, imprisonments, and records to be expunged. Additionally, those who have fallen victim to the system need to be blessed, and set up for success.

- Formally call an end to "Operation War On Drugs" (OWOD) and recognize the wisdom found in bringing another end to Prohibition.

- Freedom to Choose for yourself will be Restored.

66.

RIGHT TO LIFE

- As soon as it is discovered that Life Exists within the womb, it is entitled to ALL Rights to Life, and Protections of it, as afforded by our Creator, and detailed in our Bill of Rights, and U.S. Constitution.

- Conception Connections, and the Adoption Options can be created as alternatives to our present practice of abortion through Operation Planned Parenthood (OPP).

67.

SECOND AMENDMENT

- Your Right to Keep and Bear Arms, shall not be infringed.

- Minimize off-limit areas (Restriction zones) within America.

- Minimal areas are off-limits from Second Amendment Rights, carry except on someone else's private property (their decision)—However, if this Right has been restricted it then becomes the property owner's Responsibility to provide for the protection of their patrons (in the case of business) also face the legal ramifications for falling short.

- Illuminate the TRUTH about firearms with the facts—cities with freer gun rights are safer, period. Compare the numbers, and then do the math.

- Second Amendment must be restored to our soldiers, both on and off duty. Common sense tells us that Our Soldiers and Service-members should be expected to be carrying a firearm while in uniform, just as an officer does. A soldier is a soldier 100% of the time. Terrorism places them directly in the crosshairs of our enemies. They must be able to defend against and decimate their attackers at home, as well as abroad. Our defenders of freedom must be trustworthy enough to carry personal offense/defense measures, around the clock. 18 year olds who have enlisted in the Armed Forces would therefore also be entitled to this provision.

- After the military, Citizenry has right to first-dibs on ammunition during times of national shortage (over DHS, NSA, TSA, ATF, CIA, FBI, IRS, INS, Etc.).

- Gun records kept by the government must be expunged.

- We have the Right to Privacy.
- Serial numbers not required.
- No federal tax stamps.
- No federal small arms bans tolerated

- The Right to Keep and Bear Arms shall NOT be infringed upon, even in your personally owned vehicle (it is an extension of self). Therefore, All American commuters maintain the right to protect themselves while within their vehicles, and therefore are entitled to exercise their Second Amendment Rights without special permission.
- However, certain restrictions would apply to those granted amnesty, refugees, and newly naturalized citizens on a provisional basis.

SECURITY

- We must not give up our Freedom in the name of security. Ben said it best.

- In order to ensure All Our Rights are protected, We must find a Moral Balance between Freedom and Security that weighs heavily on the side of Freedom.
- Balance pivots on the actual dangers, the enemy, and the seriousness of the threat.

- Various areas of security, each requiring its own balance:

    - Technology
    - Military
    - Healthcare
    - Personal
    - Business
    - Wall Street
    - Industrial
    - Etcetera

- We will bring about an end to government intrusion.
- Any surveillance tools that we have can be lase- focused on tracking proven criminals—especially focused on sex criminals, murderers, and Jihadists, for example.
- Any illegal activity discovered during the normal legal course of surveillance must

be ignored entirely and destroyed, this because of the necessity to protect Americans' Right to Privacy, and right to discourage warrantless searches and seizures.

- Establish a Whistleblower's Constitutional Defense League (WCDL)—Run by The People, working closely with the Inspector General, and to be Perpetually funded.

69.

SEPARATION OF CHURCH AND STATE

- Intrusion exists when the government makes laws and regulates faith anywhere, anywhen, and anyway. For example, at football games, military school, church sermons (demanding copies, filing lawsuits, etcetera).

- We live in a Judeo-Christian Nation. That IS what our legal system is based upon. That IS a Fact.

- There will be NO legal form of Sharia law practiced within The United States of America.

- There will be NO loudspeaker playing of religious prayer services that violate the personal space of others, and/or incites riotous disturbance, among the otherwise peaceful Americans.

- The government steps in when one religion abuses another religion, or people.

70.

SEX OFFENDERS / STRANGER KIDNAPPERS / PEDOPHILES

- No second-chances for sex offenders, stranger kidnappers, violent kidnappers, and all pedophiles since their recidivism rate is near 100%.

- Those who are convicted of the above offenses have a mental and moral disorder that incarceration cannot cure. For that reason alone, the government has the responsibility to its citizens to remove these types of predators from society, permanently.

- Establish a federal one-strike law. Mandatory Life Sentence and/or Death Penalty, for the aforementioned.

71.

SMALL BUSINESS / NEW BUSINESS

- Assess the current situation.
- Recognize the massive benefit new and small businesses provide to our country.
- Provide relief and assistance when and if needed.
- Establish a perpetually funded, user-directed, Small Business Outlet for efficiency.
- Remove the prohibitive red tape that is keeping many Americans from beginning their new start up.
- Simplify taxation, and vote in a simple Flat Tax Rate for businesses, and have our government work with the proceeds from a fair taxation system.
- Reduce barriers to entry.

72.

SPORTS MEDICINE EXPERTS

- Experts required to participate and over-watch public / government / military athletics programs
- Incorporate sports medicine expertise within the military setting, at the lowest efficient level.
- Incorporate proven international, multicultural techniques, wisdom, etc.
- Incorporate naturopathic/homeopathic methodology when appropriate.
- Enforce higher standards regarding our of preventive medicine approach within the combat setting.

73.

SOCIAL SECURITY

- Vote to keep it or to dismantle it.

If we choose to keep it:

- We must keep our promises to all investors.
- Provide for opt-out, and full refund, options.
- Allow for opt-back-in options.
- Provide for a cash-out early option, or refund, that includes payment on interest, of a similar rate that our government charges those who are late in their tax payments.
- Allow for tax-exempt transfer of benefits to any individual the investor chooses.
- Utilize social security numbers for voting purposes (especially online).
- It would need to be cut free from Federal ties, and run by the Will of The People.
- Your Social Security Number (SSN) IS your identification number.

74.

SOCIAL SERVICES

- We, The People have the right to privacy—and therefore we have the right to refuse interaction with social services without a court order.
- Right to not be harassed
- Refusal to receive social-services must be respected by provider unless a serious crime has been committed
- Removing children from their parents and families must be our absolute last remedy when seeking to correct difficult situations that arise.
- Social services Will shift to an entity that assists needy individuals in getting what they need—and Will act as a welfare, healthcare, vehicular, immigration, etcetera, with system-navigators who are opportunity advocates, proficient at helping Americans get the answers they need, and the access to the resources available to them.
- Social services will not have any fee-charging nor law-setting authority
- Constitutional Rights courses required for all federal and social service employees.

75.

STATES' RIGHTS

- When Our Constitution was established, states were seen as sovereign and individual. As such, states (seen much like countries) do enjoy the rights that are laid out in Our Constitution, Declaration of Independence, and Bill of Rights.

- Federal government is the glue that brings U.S. together, and Unites U.S. in common cause, laws, and defense. Federal government needs not necessarily be more powerful than the states it Unites.

- United We Stand, divided We fall.

- States rights must be protected from Federal overreach.

- States expected and required to challenge all unconstitutional laws, until such laws have been corrected have been ratified by the common consent of The People.

76.

STOCK TRADING WHILE IN PUBLIC OFFICE

- Is a major source of corruption.
- Presents a significant conflict of interest.
- Financial assets must be frozen while in office.
- Future financial gains monitored for possible link to corruption
- Insider trading outlawed (or legalized) for All people, especially those We elected.

77.

TAXES & INHEIRITANCES

- Temporarily, individualized tax filing will not be necessary.
- Taxation through Federal Reserve printing until after the Jubilee.
- Everyone temporarily pays through inflation

- Return to the gold standard, will be a process.
- When money exchanged for gold, cash will be destroyed.
- Federal expenses will be severely cut.

- Use of Perpetualized investments coupled with a hand-over, and hand-off type of approach to the creation of, and maintenance of, social services, welfare, education, healthcare, and other outlets.

- Social Security optional, transferrable, and early withdraw-able (if We keep it).
- Government not entitled to the property of any dying individual, unless that individual expressly offers their property to the government.

- Elimination of cyclical property taxes.
- Elimination of duplicate taxation placed on any object/service/electronic media.

78.

TECHNOLOGY / FCC / EMP/ RADIOWAVES

- We have a Moral Obligation, and Responsibility to be truthful and transparent with Our People, in order to maintain a nation of informed citizens.

- Responsibility to incorporate basic protections from power surges, EMPs, solar flares, and sabotage.
- As a public security measure we will mandate the incorporation of Electro-Magnetic Pulse (EMP) defense into all new and existing publicly used infrastructure, electronics, vehicles, homes, and electricity grids. This policy would effectively nullify the FCCs' mandate that all consumer electronics be able to accept unwanted incoming signals that could cause undesirable performance.
- Incorporate Radio Wave shielding on all new homes and new roofing materials

- Government has the responsibility to identify and clean up new and existing radio pollution, and must implement policies that work to shield the individual from damaging radio pollution.
- Businesses directed to incorporate radio wave pollution protections for their employees and patrons.

- Snooping technology within consumer products must be openly disclosed, be controllable by the consumer, and be "Rated" for intrusiveness on original packaging and documentation, and must be made freely available to the consumer.
- Have electronic "firewall-filters" developed which defend the individual from unwanted incoming and outgoing signals, information and spying, from occurring while at home or on the go
- No snooping technology allowed in children's toys without express parental consent.
- All tracking features must be user disable-able, and have a physical on/off switch.

- Electronic, and mass-application mind-control technology outlawed for use in America, and upon Americans (please refer to MKULTRA).
- Subliminal, and Psychological Operations (PsyOps) illegal for use in America, and upon Americans, period.

- We must be allowed to technologically advance in order for U.S. to regain position in Our global neighborhood. Everyone knows that Our government has stood in the way of increased technological progress, specifically in the arena of new energy options, vehicular travel, and communications. This new policy will undo all of that.

- Americans have the right to have be notified of, and have access to ExtraTerrestrial Technology (ETT) when discovered.
- Patent process assessed and streamlined for ease of the common inventor and common good.

- Removal of most barriers that have been established by the Federal Communications Commission (FCC) saving only the most serious/sensitive commonsense policies/rules.
- FCC to be transformed into the Public Oversight Outlet (POO) and will become into a public facilitator, operated by the general public, whose purpose would be to advise, assist, and make recommendations—a sort of fusion hub for all things technology—all such services provided by the POO would be free from fees/fines. The existing FCC would be ultimately stripped of its power, and that power would reside within Our judicial system, where the courts can be depended on to sort out serious issues that arise.
- Offer high tech assistance to those who are seeking to create new and ingenious technological advances that show promise.

79.

TERM LIMITS / BROKEN TRUST / ACCOUNTABILITY

- Broken trust by elected officials, law enforcement, attorneys, and judges needs to be restored quickly, and can be, by taking several steps. Those who are in positions of public trust need to have their records of work performed, and judgments made, tickets written, etc., etc., simplified, and made available to the public for easy, open review.
- Collectively—the voice of the people can and will be heard. Petitions for removal from office where needed, and investigations can be initiated into accusations of corruption and other unjust practices, allowing for rapid discovery and correction.

- No individual should be afforded the opportunity to gain and exercise unjust power, dominion, nor influence over Our People and Our global Neighbors.

- I suggest we incorporate term limits for all publicly elected positions of trust and authority.

- Together we can get to the Truth, and defend our constitutionally protected Human Rights.

- This system will provide for rapid recognition and identification of rogue trust-breakers, and assist in their speedy removal.

TERRORISM / TERRORISTS

- All who shed innocent blood need to be identified as terrorists, the common enemy to Our Way of Life.

- Our policy towards terrorism must be one of complete abhorrence, and rapid response by our military once positively identified. All such acts of innocent blood shedding can and will be actively investigated and remedied by the military when linked with a religious cause.

- Any action taken must be rapid, precise, effective, and human-cost effective.

- All who stand with U.S. and accept Our Terms, Including participation in the Jubilee, may be welcomed into our Alliance.

- I do NOT believe in the practice of Catch-and-Release, when we are dealing with terrorists. This practice only helps to facilitate their evil designs.

- Remove the "Leash" which holds back our military, and allow them to do what needs to be done, when it requires combat action.

- Defend U.S, Israel, and our Alliance. Annihilate all who threaten Our Lives, and the lives of the Innocent.

- Monitor and respond to all communications related to jihadist terrorism.

81.

TRAVELLERS' RIGHTS (AIR, BUS, RAIL)

- Right to 2nd Amendment protections remain in effect when travelling.
- If no protection is being provided within publicly available commercial travel options, then citizens need to be afforded the ability to defend themselves and carry their loaded firearms.

- We Demand our Moral Right to personal privacy. It's not the government's responsibility to track and catalog each individual's travel choices.

- Right to travel with cash undeclared, any amount (right to privacy) is protected.
- Right to not be X-rayed, nor be subjected to see-thru technology is protected.
- Right to not be manhandled is protected.
- Right to travel unmolested and without detention, without just cause, or just compensation for the misdeed or delay is demanded.

- Right to safe public transportation experience (security must be provided) is demanded.
- Right to expect, and to receive standard, quality minimums, during air, bus, and rail transportation.

- We have the Right to a full refund if cancelling a ticket purchase within 24 hours of departure or 12 hours since ticket purchase, (whichever is later).

- If the traveller is a citizen, travelling within our nation, then they do not have to answer questions regarding the reason for their travel. They are not to be questioned and searched and seized as if they are criminals, that is, unless they ARE proven criminals.

TRUTH SUPPRESSION & PROPAGANDA

- Propaganda used within the United States, and On We, The People, must be, and will be immediately outlawed.

- Truth and transparency is a fundamental requirement of all governing officials. In and out of office.

- Government officials are to be considered under oath while in office 24 hours a day, 7 days a week.

- Simplify the process for speedy removal of corrupted individuals and policies.

83.

TRUTH UNIVERSITY

- This would be place to study Truth in American and Earth history, with unprecedented access to first-hand historical documents and data.

- Focus on the teachings and beliefs of our founding fathers and their principles, documents, and actions, and Our Relationship with the God of Abraham, Isaac, and Jacob, etcetera.

- It would be a place for All People, everywhere, and everywhen, to get a Constitutional foundation in the Biblical, Moral, Ethical, Truthful, Evidenced based, God factors that are necessary for society to persist as a Free People, especially true for North America.

- Future world leaders would be encouraged to take courses, and/or graduate from this university since it would show "We The People" that they have been taught in Truth, and provided with documented American principles, where the Constitution is Learned, Studied and Revered.

- Elected officials can then be held to that higher standard.

- Require continuing education (CEs) for all elected officials, to be taken directly from this university. Then, hold these elected officials to the standard they Now have a history of proven understanding.

84.

UNIDENTIFIED FLYING OBJECTS (UFOs) & EXTRATERRESTRIALS (ETs)

- Provide truthful transparency and provide factual evidence to Who, What, When, Where, and Whys related to this conspiracy.

- Support freedom of information

- Support demystification

- Support publics' Right to Be Informed

- Support integration of discovered technology into public arena as free use information.

- Provide full disclosure.

UNITED STATES CONSTITUTION

- The U.S. Constitution provides U.S. the foundation for the American Dream and is THE Supreme Law of the Land.

- It's time We reset this system and return to THE Founding Principles found within our Constitution. I believe it is time to look to our ancestors for the answers to our present-day problems, and to return to our roots, being firmly planted in Truth, Principle, Character, Freedom, Liberty, Justice, and having Faith in THE God of Abraham, Isaac, and Jacob.

- If We wish to survive this and remain a FREE PEOPLE, The Constitution IS the system we can return to since, over time, We have lost our way.

- It's time for the removal of outdated, useless, unjust laws
- It's time to incorporate expiration dates for any newly ratified laws, by mandating regular review and ratification if it is a law we wish to keep.

- It's time to establish a perpetually funded Constitutional Rights Defense Association (CRDA) for the benefit of We, The People that is run by The People.

- Suggest We vote to completely restore our laws to that of Washington's time, with all current amendments remaining, except for (by vote) amendments which change the way government does business, for example, senators would be appointed again, by elected representatives of each state. We would continue to maintain term limits on the presidency and also apply term limits to Our Congress positions.

- 8 years is more than enough time for any one individual to push their agenda.

- Absolute power corrupts absolutely.

86.

VETERANS

- You have the Right to a pension

- You have the Right to be paid first, prior to all other debts being paid by the Federal Government.

- You have the Right to Keep and Bear Arms. No special licensing required.

- You have the Right to have your service record converted into an accredited degree without extra schooling, and be based upon your proficiency, leadership, efficiency, and advancement and learning.

- You have the Right to have your healthcare provided for, both during and after service to Our Nation.

- You have the Right to affordable land and available Land Grants.

- You have the Right to return to active duty, at any age, if you can meet all other requirements.

- You have the Moral Obligation to speak Truth openly.

87.

VOTING & CHILDREN'S RIGHT TO REPRESENTATION

- Technology can provide U.S. with a cost effective, simplified approach to elections, utilizing our social security numbers (SSNs) for accountability. Virtual receipts would be provided, and a record of voting history would be compiled for protection of the system and historic integrity.

- I suggest we use modern encryption technology, and our SSNs to authenticate individuals and allow Americans to vote from the comfort of their homes.

- This approach to voting would save time and money by reducing the need for polling locations, monitoring, etc. And, this approach would increase participation in all elections.

- I believe all lives matter, especially the lives of our Children. I support amending the constitution to allow parents to vote in proxy for their children. For example, a family with two parents and three children under the legal age of eighteen would have five votes to cast in each election. When spouses differ in their views, their votes can be divided equally.

88.

WELFARE

- Support the establishment of a perpetually funded welfare fund run by The People.

- Made available to all U.S. Citizens, and non-citizens alike.

- It will be simplified, centralized, networked and efficient.

- Establish free Public Access Outlets (PAO) for the following:

    - Healthcare
    - Emergency care
    - Dentalcare
    - Rehabilitation
    - Recovery
    - Counseling
    - Employment
    - Educational counseling
    - Food
    - Shelter
    - Showers and Sanitization
    - Tent/RV provisions
    - Veterinary services

- Charitable contributions encouraged

WOMEN'S RIGHTS / EQUALITY & RESPONSIBIILTIES

- By now it should be patently obvious to U.S. that Woman are equal to Men, and Women have the unique ability to produce human offspring.

- Women have the Responsibility to rear their offspring according to the dictates of their own conscience, or offer them up for adoption.

- Therefore, Women have the Right to equal pay, and opportunities, based upon equal performance

- Women have the Right to Safety and Security from abusive men.

- Women have the right to rule their own bodies, and they have the moral obligation and responsibility to protect their unborn children.

- The child that grows within a woman's womb is a separate entity and therefore has Equal Rights to that of their mother. Once conception has occurred, the unborn child IS HUMAN, and has the right to life, just as its mother.

- Women have the right to not have their children taken from them by any entity, without due process.
- Ideally, the mother and father would raise their Children together, but Women can choose to give their Child to another—through adoption. However, the Child's Father is next in line to raise his Children.

- A Woman can choose to terminate her pregnancy, but that termination cannot result in the death of her unborn Child. Emerging technology and advances in medicine will likely allow for the transfer of the growing Child from one Woman to another.

- Adoption services to be made a free public service. (Promote the common welfare).

90.

WORLD CURRENCY

- It's my position that no fiat world currency would be wise to enter into exchange with. However returning to the usage of trade dollars coined in gold and silver (and other precious metals or commodities and/or services).
- We will NOT engage in trade with Our People's enemies.

PLEASE JOIN U.S.
AS WE STAND
IN THE GAP

In addition to the aforementioned, I would like to openly declare the following:

We, The People, of these United States of America do hereby extend our hand of friendship to our global family (neighbors) and to each individual, individually, throughout the world. We recognize that you, and All people everywhere are truly our brothers and sisters.

We are from the same human family and we share almost identical DNA. This should make it clear to All that we see you for what you are, a person made in God's image, priceless, even though your governments might not be.

If you are Jewish, Christian, or Kurdish, and are facing genocide, We will Stand for you, and we will sweep your enemies into that annals of Hell. We share a common enemy. We will not sit and watch history to repeat itself as genocide sweeps the planet. Every minute we lose, innocent lives are being taken, Men, Women, and even young Children are being raped, tortured, decapitated, burned, drowned, hanged, and even crucified, for what cause?

America is better than this.

Because our global neighborhood has suffered so much hardship due to the corruption of our elected officials and its extensions, AND We have failed to stop those who propagate corruption, I believe it right that We offer our sincerest apologies to our Allies especially, and ask for their patience and understanding as We restore our Republic (this is not a kowtow). We ask that they know that their Friendship, Patience, Love, Compassion, Charity, Understanding, and Assistance will be rewarded in kind.

As Mahatma Gandhi United India and Helped to loose their bands of servitude and subjection through the application of Peaceful Resistance and Expression, together, WE, The People, must, and will do the same. We will All be Gandhi, We will All be Martin Luther King, We will All stand to restore and reunite our country, and our global alliance. Everyone has important work to perform. Everyone who can and is able is needed to assist in bringing about this great restoration, and ultimately, The Great American Reunion.

WE HEREBY DECLARE Hope, Peace, and Goodwill towards All people, everywhere, and ask All People to share this message and to assist U.S. in this great undertaking. We must turn our hearts to THE God of Abraham, Isaac, and Jacob, ask for His forgiveness, express charity towards All People, express the Love We have in Our Hearts for one another, Rescue the Oppressed, and defend All Life. It is only then that We will have the Peace, Freedom, Liberty and Security All Americans desire.

If you can believe in the power of God and HIS Ability to Magnify the Abilities of HIS Children (the individual), and if you can Believe that your voice and your vote does in fact count, *and* if the vision I'm presenting for our future Resonates within your Heart, please join with U.S. in spreading this message of Hope, and getting the word out that someone (Patrick Anthony Ockander) has finally stepped up who is Of The People, and For The People, who will do the Will of The People, no matter what.

It is my humble belief that the vision I propose herein is one that you would be willing to Represent. This vision makes sense; in fact, it is LOADED with Common Sense. If allowed to be implemented this vision is one that can reunite U.S. all, reestablish our Individual Sovereignty, reestablish the Sovereignty of the State, and place the will of The People back where it should be, in control of our Republic.

DECLARATION OF INDEPENDENCE

We, The People, do hereby re-declare our International independence, and do also express our extreme dissatisfaction with Our Tyrannical, out of control politicians. We demand that our U.S. Constitution be fully restored, and that unconstitutional and outdated laws be immediately invalidated.

REVIEW OF WORKS

We, The People demand that all sitting politicians submit to a public assessment of their histories; determining inconsistencies, unethical behavior, unconstitutional actions if there be any.

RESELECTION BY POPULAR VOTE

Where and when corruption is found, immediate removal from office must be forthwith, and the individual must be subjected to a thorough investigation into their fraudulent or subversive activity.

THE FOCUS

In removing a corrupt official from their seat of power, it must remain We, The People's focus to reduce the harm inflicted by these corrupt individuals, and to actively seek their replacement with trustworthy representatives who are willing to serve U.S. Honorably.

They need not be politicians, or overly experienced, but most importantly, they need to be honest individuals who are determined to place the will of The People above their own personal aspirations.

Punishment of corrupt politicians needn't be our focus. It is better to show compassion towards these misguided individuals, and provide them with pathways towards forgiveness and restitution. We will ask for their help in repairing the damage they inflicted by exposing their role, and "whistleblowing" in lieu of incarceration. We'll see Heroes made from what we thought was chaff...Edward Snowden, for example.

Edward Snowden did U.S. all a great service by exposing the deceit and deep violations against our Constitution, and Our Trust. Corruption and civil rights abuses had become standard operating procedure among our ruling politicians. Patriot Edward Snowden deserves to be openly thanked and rewarded for his Courage to do the hard thing, knowing beforehand the Great Personal Sacrifice he would be required to endure. Patriot Snowden deserves total restoration of his place in Our Society, and have his Freedom and his possessions restored to him, and to have his name chiseled in Our Nation's history and folklore, for being today's Paul Revere.

Elimination of corruption within our government, and selection/cultivation of honest and trustworthy leaders who are determined to stand for the U.S. Constitution during times of adversity, and who are willing to best represent their constituents through honesty and integrity, must be our focus.

WE EXPECT BAD NEWS

Trustworthy leaders will know that maintaining the confidence of their constituency and working within the framework of Our Constitution are expected and that, so called, "bad news", or embarrassing disclosures, will be met with objectivity and understanding.

So tell U.S. the truth. Be honest, direct, and forthcoming with U.S. We hired you, We pay you. You were hired to serve U.S. Do Our Will, or go home. This isn't about you and your personal quest for fame, fortune, and power. It's about U.S., it's about Freedom, and it's about speaking the Truth, especially when it's most difficult.

THE LITMUS TEST

All elected servants must be able to answer Yes or No when asked simple, direct questions. If they can't do that in the primaries, then they can't be expected to do so if they were elected. We must not allow such politicians to represent U.S.

THE GREAT RESTORATION

Because of the great corruption we are currently facing, I suggest we exert our efforts to restore the U.S. Constitution to the time of George Washington, whilst subjecting our amendments to a thorough review. Then, when done, by consensus we can determine which amendments to keep and which ones to nullify, and what new amendments need to be established to keep a future tyranny from reoccurring. Obviously we won't be returning to the practice of indentured servitude nor slavery.

SUPREME COURT

All Supreme Court justices' records and actions will be subjected to a thorough review. I suggest a total reset of this system, and in addition, each justice needs to be individually sustained by We, The People prior to being allowed to pass judgment.

LAWS

I believe it's time to expire all laws outside our founding documents that are over 100 years old, and immediately place 5-year expiration dates on all remaining laws. Understanding that if the law is important enough to be maintained, then it needs to be re-ratified every 10 years by congress, and if the law is important enough to maintain for a longer duration, and to be excluded from this process, then the Constitution needs to be amended to represent these exclusions.

A GLIMPSE INTO THE FUTURE

As this effort unfolds, committees will be formed, and Honest Experts from all fields called in, and upon, to assist in this great corrective/restorative undertaking.

Congress will be expected to take on a selfless service type approach, and be expected to put in long hours (at least 40 hours a week). If We, The People, normally work 40-hour weeks, then our governing elected officials can be expected to do the same. Also, the practice of congress drinking alcohol (on the job) during work hours will no longer be permitted.

Application of technological advances through the adaptation of many of society's needs into straightforward internet platforms will allow We, The People to directly engage and participate in all aspects of the governing spectrum, and access government services, fee-free. This will help to reduce corruption, increase patriotic participation, and reduce costs associated with employment of a massive government workforce, as well it will stimulate an overall reduction in costs associated with the maintenance of all the massive infrastructure currently required for today's day to day federal business.

ELIMINATE OR HANDOVER ALL NON-ESSENTIAL FEDERAL ROLES TO THE PUBLIC

A massive reduction in government spending, federal overreach, oversight, and the expensive time-consuming, bureaucratic spider-web We are all forced to suffer through, can occur by transfer of authority and management from the Federal level Up and over to those who are vigilant within he American public.

Once responsibility has been transferred, the Fed simply lets go and steps back to allow the will of The People to be exercised through individual, local interactions and elections of board members, establishment of bylaws, votes, etcetera. All the while, complete oversight and interaction is available directly to the public, as well as to the Federal government.

Excepting State Secrets, Transparency of all governing entities, public services, legal processes, and procedures, etc., will be made immediately available for video review, and will be made available to be scrutinized with the severest level of, oversight and public interaction that is beneficial to society's needs.

SURVEILLANCE

This brings up the need to shift the government's policy of public surveillance and their invasion of Our Privacy, to one that limits the government's usage of this technology within America, and in turn redirects the focus back to those who have been elected to govern The United States of America, those who have a proven track record of violence, crime, subversion, abuse, pedophilia, conspiracy, rape, and murder, or who have made verifiable threats against the life, liberty, property, or pursuit of happiness of other individuals.

ENDING THE DRUG WAR

Spending will continue to fall, and freedom be increased when the Constitution is amended to reflect the sovereignty of the individual to choose if they ingest any substance, or not. For protections to be established for All People, even if their pursuit of happiness choices to ingest or not to ingest one substance or another, or food, or immunization, or medication, or not. And, these individuals have the right to have their personal expressions of conscience respected and tolerated by the government and The People.

INDIVIDUAL FREE WILL

The free will of one individual doesn't diminish the free will of another. Do no harm. And if one chooses to harm another, then the severe repercussions should follow. And so on and so forth...With this brief summary I invite you to review my proposal in its entirety and decide for yourself if you could support this Patriot, and if you can, then please join me and spread the word.

CLIMATE GATE

"Every thought we think emanates around the world," therefore think charitable thoughts.

Our common enemy would have you believe you are destroying the earth, that you are the cause of all the calamities and weather variations. I tell you that this is not entirely true. For, remember, "Ye are the salt of the earth", meaning you are good for Earth, like salt is good for a man. There are extremes that *do* inflict harm on our planet, but these extremes amount to a very small percentage.

There are however, those who, with forethought and malevolence, sabotage Our otherwise safe practices of collecting and processing oil other natural resources, and they do this to assist with their deception.

SOMETHING SPIRITUAL

Have faith that you, the individual, can and are able to have a Major Positive Influence (MPI) on this experience we are all sharing in. CHOOSE Your Own Adventure and make your life the greatest story ever written. Prepare for your Return to our Father in Heaven, with honor, and with open arms.

Love everyone. Abhor evil. Hate nobody, and no thing.

Be like Mahatma Gandhi.

Be like Jesus of Nazareth.

Accept that you are who you are, in this very moment, so Be Good. Remember that you DO make a difference. Seek to discover your calling, and then take action to fulfill it.

Know that a single hour of inner work will produce the same result as seven hours of actual physical work. Thinking is effective, so think.

And Pray.

While taking care of a patient of mine who was actively dying of cancer, I was sitting at his desk when I noticed a cartoon posted to the wall. It explained that there are two types of Men in this world. One type of man seeks the constant incarceration of his Brethren, whereas the other type of Man continually seeks to set his Brethren and Sisters free. I am the type of man who seeks to set my Brothers and Sisters free.

REHABILITATION VERSUS INCARCERATION

Consider this. Maybe we can begin to focus on ways to persuade men to do good by recognizing the individual (who has, may, or is going astray) and seek to entice them to do good by enlightening them and by providing them with opportunities to find happiness and camaraderie through goodness, rather than destructive means.

For example, imagine an inner-city young man who has never been outside his immediate environment, never seen the ocean, never heard the sound of waves crashing on the shore, nor spent an afternoon atop a beautiful mountain.

A young man like this would likely enjoy the excitement and tranquility of outdoor motorsports, dirt-biking, snowmobiling, hunting, fishing, and building a cabin, etcetera.

If We were to take an individual that is on a destructive pathway and provide him with a wholesome alternative, like the aforementioned, rather than simply imprisoning him, it would be much more beneficial to him, his family, and to society as a whole. After the introduction to a healthy alternative lifestyle, and removal from his immediate environment (relocation), career and opportunity counselors can be deployed to assist the individual in finding a career path or opportunity that fits his personality and desires.

OUR NATIONAL PARKS AND RESOURCES

One problem Americans face is that Our natural resources and our national parks are all tied up in fences and entangled in a bureaucratic web of regulations and restrictions that directly restrict We, The People, from the very outdoor activities that many Americans enjoy, or would enjoy if allowed the opportunity.

When I was younger I Loved to hike, bike, dirt bike, camp, explore, and jog regularly. There was a large ranch that existed nearby Our childhood home that was privately owned, and was off-limits, patrolled, and seldom used by its owners.

This property has long since changed hands, and is now a state park, a neighborhood, and an apartment complex, the natural side (greenbelt) is still off-limits to many of the activities that We, The People enjoy.

I was told that the reason We were regularly run off the property was because our dirt biking was damaging the property...after some time, bulldozers came in and completely changed the landscape. Protecting nature was never the issue.

I don't see the wisdom in restricting Our People from accessing Our Land. Why aren't we allowed to explore, drive our vehicles, and even find hidden treasure on these lands? Why has that excitement been totally killed off? Why have We, The People become so restricted to use the lands we Love so much? And, why do we have to pay to play? Why does it seem that almost any activity We want to engage in has to come with additional costs, fees, fines, restrictions and policing? Where is the freedom in that? It seems to me We have been collectively corralled, and controlled, and forced into tiny little boxes squished side by side to one another for way too long.

ANOTHER LAND RUSH

There is enough land for all of U.S. to go around. If we all have charity in our hearts we can share this land, cultivate it, and assist one another in this endeavor.

I propose that We share this land, and use it. In fact, if elected, I support the reallocation of these lands to the people. I support allowing for land grants for All Americans, and allow Americans to explore much of our nationally "owned" parks, find a spot of land, of an appropriate size for their needs, and allow We, The People to build upon it. Establish Our homes, on or off the grid, and allowing for individual ownership of the property so long as they maintain it and keep it.

A WORD ON TAXATION

I propose that we do away with the way taxation has been traditionally done. Today it is a form of clever enslavement. I say let's do away with it. We can use the Federal Reserve to our advantage as we phase back into a gold standard and repurpose/dismantle the Reserve.

Today Our Federal Reserve prints the money it can't get from Americans through quantitative easing and lack of powerful regulation. If the reserve can simply print the money it needs, why then do we have individual taxation at all?

I say we temporarily use the Federal Reserve to print the money our society needs, and we will all pay a fair share through inflation, UNTIL we have had the Jubilee and have been safely returned to the gold standard, and have established a simple Flat Tax Rate (FTR) that All Americans pay Equally. Simply.

I believe that by keeping taxes low and simple, equal for all citizens, and mandating that the Federal government work within the budget we have allotted them, We can restore Power to The People. I believe this is the Moral thing to do.

WIRETAPPING

I also propose that we halt the practice of continual spying on We, The People, and instead increase Privacy and availability to remain anonymous.

I would like to see the power of our technology and surveillance turned around on those who are presently in control of it. I'd like to see our government under the same type of scrutiny that We are all currently facing now.

A LITTLE BIT ABOUT ME

My name is Patrick Anthony Ockander, it's pronounced, "O-Candor".

Many of my friends know me by my nickname "Tony", especially those who know me from Southern California. Others may know me only by my last-name, due to that's the way people refer to each other while in the military (and that's what's affixed to your uniform). Still, there are many who know me by my given name, Patrick (especially those from San Antonio, Spokane, Coeur 'd Alene, DC, and Tacoma). A few variations of my name were used during my years in elementary and high school. Some of these variations included "Tone'", "Toné", and even "Mr. Ockander". Some of the stranger names I've gone by include, "Doc", "Ock", "Doc-Ock", "Medic!", "Soldier Medic", "Candyman", "Bonus", "Tonus", "Tonus 'R Bonus", "Red", and even, "my social security number, or the last four.

I was conceived in the back of a 1973 Chevy pickup, in cab-over camper in Calabasas, California, on a road that no longer exists, but when it did it was called "Quintana". I was born June 8th, 1975 in Panorama City, California. I grew up in the city of Calabasas (means squash, or gourd). It's nestled in a small canyon known as Malibu Canyon (means loud crashing wave) not far from Pepperdine University. It is here and near to here where I enjoyed most of my youth.

I believe I've been uniquely prepared for this undertaking, that my life has been guided in such a way as to prepare me for this very endeavor. I have never felt so up to a challenge as I do now.

In the spirit of Truth and Transparency, I want to begin by sharing with you a personal story that is sacred to me and that, until now, has been shared with a very select few.

During my adolescent years, I was critically challenged with severe depression. At the time it was all going on I didn't know what to make of it, these dark feelings of despair, loneliness, and self-loathing haunted me, yet with hindsight I've come to realize the depression I was suffering with was likely due to my failure to live my life to the high standard expected of me, according to my understanding of Latter Day Saint (LDS) gospel doctrine.

That, coupled with feelings of failure, a broken heart, damaged important friendships, low self-esteem, slow growth, raging hormones, early exposure to sex, and a lot of chaos in a home filled with Attention Deficit Hyperactivity Disorder (ADHD) a tired Firefighter Dad, and a Mom continually stretched to her limits with 6 kids.

This depression I went through began when I was about 11 or 12 years old, and continued on until one serious event changed everything for me at about 18 years old.

I was a young high school graduate, with everything going for me, yet I was plagued with severe depression that I couldn't snap out of. I falsely believed nobody else could relate to what I was feeling. I had supportive family and friends that tried to help me through this real-life drama. Eventually I became determined to take my life.

In desperation, I began experimenting with drugs, believing the media propaganda that using drugs would kill you. Yet, as hard as I tried, I continued to live. Since that wasn't working I came up with the plan to overdose on sleeping pills, and the several times I attempted, rather than expire, I'd fall asleep for some unknown length of time...wake up in the cold of the night, stars overhead, somewhere in the hills near my childhood home...I'd be covered in prickly weeds and hallucinating things like snakes striking at me constantly, along with other frightening things...this would go on for hours and hours.

Each time, my family and friends would miraculously find me wandering aimlessly somewhere, take me home and nurse me back to reality. I know this was a challenging time for them all. I remember being sincerely sorry for hurting so many people, and this fact only seemed to add to my resolution to stop the pain for good.

Understandably, I wasn't in any condition to have a girlfriend, and when that drama finally ended, I added a broken heart, an angry best friend, and several other damaged friendships to give me more reason to be depressed.

I decided to drive my green 1971 VW Squareback off of Kanan Road in Southern California. Most locals knew, or had heard, that Kanan Road was dangerous, and there had been several individuals who had gone off the road and over the cliffs, resulting in their deaths. So, being somewhat of a daredevil inside anyway, I figured this would be an effective way to go.

It was December 23rd or 24th, A day or so before Christmas, after being rejected by "The One", at about midnight, I headed down Kanan Road determined to drive off the cliff.

And so I did.

I turned up the volume on my radio which had a sad Love song sung by Toni Braxton entitled "Breathe Again". Here are the lyrics at the end of the song:

> Please understand if Love
> ends
> Then I promise you, I
> promise you
> That, that I shall never
> breathe again
> Breathe again, breathe
> again
> That I shall never breathe
> again, breathe again
> That I shall never breathe

again
Breathe again, breathe
again
That I shall never breathe
again, breathe again

Quite depressing as I look back on it. But, be that as it may, it was a popular song being played on the radio at the time, and I happened to own the single. With that song playing, I headed down that winding canyon road, and accelerated that little VW as fast as it could go (which was about 80 miles per hour, maybe a little faster when going downhill) undid my seatbelt, said a little prayer, then, as I exited one of the tunnels I spotted what I thought was an ideal place to launch the car, and as the road curved to the right...I kept driving straight.

I remember several things from the event. I remember seeing a small road reflector bend over as it was struck with my car, and I remember branches being illuminated in the headlights, and could hear branches scratching and breaking just before going airborne.

I remember the darkness of the night as I was airborne, and the initial impact that made the brightest flash of white light in my mind, coupled with the loudest bang I had ever heard up till then. Maybe I was unconscious for a moment after, I don't know, but I do remember a second bang and flash of light as I impacted at least a second time, and then silence. Dead silence and total darkness.

I had instant regret, and immediately thought to myself, Tony, Tony, Tony, what have you done? Now you have to find a way out of here. There was Total darkness, extreme weakness, the salty taste of blood in my mouth, and difficulty breathing as I coughed what I believed to be blood. My vehicle was upside down, and I was crammed under the steering wheel, between the front driver's seat and the pedals.

I reached for the window and only felt dirt, followed with a sense of panic and despair, as I believed I was trapped inside a crushed car with no way out. I reached for the passenger window and felt dirt again. I thought the roof had collapsed to only a few inches, but later learned that the high back seats had acted like a roll cage and kept the roof from totally collapsing.

As my ability to remain conscious diminished, and in total despair, and extreme sorrow for my actions, and realizing that I was about to pass away, I called upon our Heavenly Father and told him how sorry I was, and I begged HIM for His Forgiveness.

As I reached out to the Lord in prayer, I remember passing out mid prayer, followed by my (immediate) presence in a very white room (so to speak, as its dimensions were unknown to me, and I couldn't see any walls).

What I also remember was audibly communing with the Lord and hearing His voice.

I did not see Him though, and cannot recollect the details of our conversation. But, the next thing I remember was being carried (levitated?) by a being that was in front of me who didn't appear or sound like he was walking as we both ascended the mountainside.

He didn't speak. I was completely paralyzed at this time, but was able to move my eyes. I saw that the figure before me appeared to be wearing a thick, dark robe, and as we moved forward and up, branches would bend and fling back, and as they brushed against his robe blue sparkles would be emitted (similar to static).

When we reached the top, the being stood by me and propped me up (without actually touching me) by the roadside. And, when the first set of headlights approached in the distance, I was released, the being disappeared and I collapsed.

I remember the kindest, most beautiful woman I had ever met coming to my aid (I still wonder who she was). I couldn't stop crying and saying "I'm sorry, I'm sorry, I'm sorry". She consoled me and asked if I had been beaten, I told her that my car had gone over the cliff. She continued to comfort me and kept me warm until the ambulance arrived. I was stripped naked and strapped to a spine board. Sent to the local Emergency Room, and put through a series of tests and examinations, X-rays, etc.

I remember being in the most severe physical pain I had Never been in. Every muscle, every joint, and every part of my body, including even my fingertips were in excruciating pain, yet not a single broken bone, and no internal injuries.

I was really thirsty but could only have a few ice chips (standard procedure). No pain medication was administered (standard procedure), and later that evening the facility wanted to discharge me, but my mother who is a Registered Nurse (RN) stood up for me and reminded them of the mechanism of injury and the need for observation.

I was discharged the following day, but before I was, I discovered I had been exposed to poison oak, and having had a history of being allergic to it, and having suffered with it several times prior, and having an idea of what was to come, I experienced an immediate sinking feeling deepening inside me. I realized I had just been GOD Smacked, and wasn't being let go scott-free.

I didn't admit it at the time, that I had purposely driven off the cliff, but I'm pretty sure my family knew what I had done, and I felt terrible about it.

The first morning after my discharge I awoke to what I thought was my older brother pushing on my shoulder, saying, "Tony, Tony, wake up", and repeating as the pushing on my shoulder with his fingertips continued, "Tony, Tony, wake up". I had been facing the wall at the time with the covers drawn up high. I lowered the covers and looked to my right and saw nobody there, and the bedroom door was closed tight. It wasn't my brother who had awakened me. I was instantly terrified.

I drew the covers up and curled into the fetal position. It happened again, "Tony, Tony, Tony, wake up", "Tony, Tony, Tony, wake up", with pushing on my shoulder. I was shaking in bed. Then, I was thrown over the foot of my bed and summersaulted into the door.

I jumped back into bed, went back to the fetal position, drew the covers up high over my head, turned to the wall, and the scenario repeated, only this time after saying my name three times, and pushing on my shoulder, twice, the words, "If you don't come to me I'm going to leave you", "If you don't come to me I'm going to leave you". With that, I was thrown out of bed again, same way as before.

As I jumped back in bed again, fetal position, with covers drawn high I shook there in silence as I contemplated the words and the events that had just transpired.

Within a day or two of my return, the poison oak I had contracted had worsened, and had begun to spread over my body. Shortly thereafter the poison oak had nearly completely covered my body with boils, blisters, oozing, crystalizing puss, and intense itching, everywhere, and I really mean everywhere.

I was completely disfigured with this affliction, and it continued on for almost exactly 365 days. I didn't leave the house much. Doctors had no remedy. My clothing consisted of white sheets. And eventually, my father and I decided to go Against Medical Advice (AMA) and go ahead and wrap my body like a mummy to isolate the exudate that was leaching from about 80-90 percent of my skin.

Day after day my father would patiently assist me with my dressing changes and compression wraps. My Father would patiently apply calamine lotion little by little over the oozing, painful, intensely itchy lesions that covered my body. My father is a very compassionate man. I will always remember this expression of Love he shared with me.

I spent the year trying to remember who I was, what my purpose is, and worked to reestablish my relationship with Heavenly Father, and my family. The fact that this poison oak lasted almost exactly a year is a testament to me of the purpose of what I was going through. It seemed to me that I was afforded an opportunity to start over, again.

There's a caveat to this story, and it comes from what my father shared with me. At the time of my hospitalization, my father, being a Visionary Man, and Humble and Honest in his nature, shared with me what he saw as I laid in my hospital bed.

He told me that as clear as he could see me laying there, he witnessed two male Angels that were very large in stature, appearing like Roman Soldiers clad with leather and armed with swords. These two Guardian Angels stood at each side of my bed and stood guard over me. My Father told me that these two Men had the most serious, determined expression on their faces. Like they were not letting anything get to me.

A lot has gone through my mind in contemplating the events of this experience. I am very thankful for my many second chances in Life. My belief that there was a purpose for my life, worth giving me a second chance for, was strengthened.

Though times weren't easy for me, I never again seriously wanted to, nor attempted to, take my life.

There were many ups and downs in my life over the next twenty years or so. I spent them working hard, playing hard, and developing many skill sets, and I gained a personal testimony regarding abortion when I was given the power to decide if my first son would be aborted or not.

Long story short, as I journeyed through the gut-wrenching process of deciding, I recognized The Spirit left me when I entertained the idea of abortion.

My first son was born in my absence in Santa Barbara, California, and was then taken to Japan. I have had very little interaction with him, but Love him dearly, and hope to establish a real relationship with him someday.

In 2003 I moved to Northern Idaho, Coeur 'D Alene, Idaho, to be precise. It's a short drive east from Spokane, Washington.

I stayed with my parents for a brief while before travelling to Malaysia and meeting my future ex-wife (to-be).

With motivation to restore honor in my life after a failed attempt at service within the Marine Corps in the 1990's (I smoked pot before basic training and didn't admit it so I got kicked out) and that, coupled with a never-ending desire to Serve and Defend our Freedom, Liberty, and Union, and seeking to successfully immigrate my future ex-wife to the states from Malaysia, and wanting to help my Brother along his difficult path by being a good example, I enlisted with the Active-duty Army in 2004.

After basic training, my specialized training as a medic, or "healthcare specialist" as it's officially termed, was performed at Fort Sam Houston, San Antonio, Texas. At that time drill sergeants controlled training. So that was not fun. Tack on more basic-training style teaching.

Fortunately, drill sergeants have now been removed from much, if not all, of this specialized training.

Once training was completed I received orders to relocate to Fort Lewis, Washington. I was assigned to I Corps, 3rd Brigade, 2nd Infantry Division (1-23 Infantry). After raking what seemed to be several tons of leaves off the I-Corps grounds, unit assimilation, more training, and lots of wasted time doing busy work, we were deployed to Baghdad, Iraq June 26, 2006 (the day my second son was born). My return to the states was in October 2007. I saw combat and I earned my Combat Medic Badge (CMB), which is arguably my proudest achievement.

I returned to Tacoma, Washington in 2007, finished out my commitment, enlisted into the Army Reserves, and was guaranteed training to become a Licensed Vocational Nurse (LVN). With a career change in focus I planned my future move, all the while battling through another war, but this war was in the home. Suffice it to say, my ex-wife and I went through major relationship, communication, international, financial, and serious mental and physical challenges that ultimately culminated in divorce.

My ex-wife returned to Malaysia, her home country, while pregnant with our daughter and accompanied with our son. Several months later our daughter was born in Kota Kinabalu, Malaysia, while we were separated.

This entire trying experience has been more difficult than words can express. I will likely discuss much of this situation in another venue, so I'll be brief. Though I won custody, I am without my children, and we have been distanced by thousands of miles, and major communication barriers.

I moved to San Antonio, TX, in 2008, and live here as of this writing. I feel at home here, but miss the California beaches, mountains, mild weather, amazing food, and old friendships. Even still, I met my wife, fell in Love, and got married. I returned to college, I've cared for the sick, injured, the wounded, the clinically insane, and the terminally ill. I have come to recognize the wonderful spirit found within the people here.

While working as an LVN, and as a member of the Army Reserves, I continued my education and ultimately graduated from The University of Texas, Health Science Center, San Antonio, School of Nursing (UTHSCSA SON) and completed my degree program in 2015.

ROOTED IN SERVICE

In reflection, I've spent much of my life in service to my fellow beings by acting on behalf of customers through advocacy, and employers through Honesty and good, efficient work. I've Lived my Life in the lower income brackets usually, though I've always had enough to be grateful.

Much of my life in service began early on within the Boy Scouts of America. Beginning at age 8, I worked my way through scouting, ultimately finishing out as a Life Scout, a notch below Eagle Scout.

I consider myself to be a True American Patriot, and I've always felt close ties with my ancestral Native American roots. I have had a deep Love, pride, respect, gratitude, and honor for the beauty of this experiment of freedom, and for our God-Blessed Country and my chance to play a part in it.

I come from a long line of patriots too. My father served in the U.S. Air Force, his father served in the US Navy, My mother's father served in the US Army, and one of my brothers is currently serving in the US Air Force as a doctor. I have another brother who left active duty after serving two tours (one to Iraq and the other to Afghanistan) and is presently serving in the Army Reserves.

In addition to these Patriots, I have several Patriot Uncles who have Honorably served within the Armed Forces too. I'm proud of my family's long history of service. I'm proud to be an American.

My father lived a life of service too. He is still married to my mother, and has faithfully supported her with the rearing of six children. He retired from the Los Angeles City Fire Department after becoming disabled, and is a

Wise Man whose life has been founded on truth and great Moral fortitude.

My Mother cared for the needs of my Father, along with the needs of her six children. She served as a homemaker, an RN, and has actively helped countless others through her many roles within the church. She is an amazing Woman, and Mother. She is patient, loving, virtuous, tender, caring, nurturing, understanding, forgiving, and talented in so many ways (for example, my brother won a Halloween costume contest dressed as a fully-set table, with his head as the centerpiece, thanks to my mom's creativity and ingenuity).

As for siblings, I have two Sisters who also live lives of service as Mothers, Wives, and nurses. I have one Brother who serves as an anesthesiologist, another Brother who is a Rad Tech, and another Brother who serves his community as a lineman in telecommunications.

Service is what I'm good at. It's what Ockanders are good at. It's what I Love, and it's what brings U.S. true happiness and sets us apart.

I was raised as a member of The Church of Jesus Christ of Latter Day Saints, a "Mormon". And no, I and We don't practice polygamy. I'm a Christian. I believe in Christ. I worship Christ. And I have been baptized in Christ's name. I have received the blessing of the gift of the Holy Ghost by the laying on of hands. I seek to emulate Christ's life to the best of my ability.

I have faith in the redeeming power of Jesus Christ, the Son of God, and of His Love for U.S., and of HIS Love and hope, and guidance for U.S. I believe in the gift of the Holy Ghost. I enjoy studying scripture, reading the Bible. I believe the Book of Mormon to be inspired of God, and believe it to be another testament of Jesus Christ. I do not believe this book replaces the Bible. I pray, I listen, and I am at peace within myself. I share this with you because it is a subject that has resurfaced time and time again, throughout my Life.

I was brought up in a somewhat diverse community, mostly tolerant of others, which included people of many different ethnicities and faiths. I developed many good friendships, and I learned much from these relationships. I came to learn first-hand of the diverse teachings that span much of the religious spectrum. I learned to respect the beliefs of others and to see the beauty found in various types of worship.

Why Seek Office?

I see the problems clearly and have solutions that will work. I believe I am being called to do this work. I recognize that most, if not all of those who are presently running don't have the answers we seek. Most candidates lack real vision, and, simply, I don't trust most of them. These politicians have burned me, like they have burned you, and they've done it too many times for me to have faith in them anymore.

Besides that, I was born for this. In an unusual way, I've spent my lifetime preparing for this. I have hope for our future. I will stand for truth. And, with your help, I know We can turn the tide of oppression.

I have eyes to see and ears to hear. I have Hope and a Vision for a brighter future, and I see the Path to Success clearly before U.S.

Plus, I'm not a politician, rather, I'm an Honest Patriot who got fed up watching from the sidelines, who decided to step up and do the hard thing.

And, I'm on God's side, are you?

I understand many of U.S. don't know who I am. Because of that fact, and my desire to be truthful and transparent with you, I'm asking everyone who has first-hand stories involving me to please share them publicly with U.S. All. I won't sue, I promise. You have it in writing here. Just please be truthful. I've also made my fair share "mistakes" and can relate to my fellow Americans. I, like my Brothers and Sisters, have watched our Freedoms gradually taken from U.S. and can see where the path We are travelling leads. Let's change Our course.

Please, if ever I've offended you, and if we've not made amends, please get in touch with me so I can seek restitution, reconciliation, and hopefully your forgiveness.

FINAL THOUGHT

I offer you my sincerest gratitude for your willingness to read this book, for your thoughtfulness, and for your consideration. Thank you. It's my hope that this Vision presented to you will be in sync with your own beliefs, that the message shared with you will resonate within U.S. all. I sincerely thank you, and pray that God will bless you, watch over you, guide and direct you, and that he will protect U.S. All.

I call upon You, the young and the old alike, as well as everyone in between. I ask you to assist me with this great undertaking. To assist in restoring our Life, Liberty, and Our ability to pursue Truth and Happiness, wherever it leads U.S.

It should now be our mission to restore the United States' Constitution and Declaration of Independence, and to restore to all the Blessings Endowed to U.S., by our CREATOR, and ESPECIALLY, to return to the FUNDAMENTAL UNDERSTANDING that the reason for our nation's many great blessings, including our place in global hierarchy, and our protections during war, are solely due to the blessings, favor, and protections granted to U.S. by our recognition, and worship of The True God, The God of Abraham, Isaac, and Jacob.

Just as Japan has Buddhism, India has Hinduism, and Haiti has Voodoo as their official religions, We, The People, founded the United States of America upon Jesus Christ's Church. The United States of America is Christian Nation.

Even still, Our Nation welcomes people of ALL FAITHS, and has established many protections of the Individual's Right to Worship according to their own personal beliefs, so long as those beliefs do not cause harm to others.

We hereby declare that the Rights afforded to U.S., that have been declared openly and discussed extensively during the founding of Our Nation, are still in effect.

If WE must, ALL 350 million of U.S. (Americans) will individually sue the Federal Government for the restoration of Our Freedoms, Our Liberties, and our Rights until the time our Freedom has been restored. It's time to Stand Up.

It's way past time for U.S. to wake up, and STAND Up for what we know is right. Let's wrap this up. STAND for U.S. and STAND for our posterity, and LET'S STAND NOW!

God Bless America!

All contributions graciously accepted.

Please visit my Facebook pages:

- Patrick Ockander
- We, The People
- The Great American Reunion
- Free Idea Up For Grab

www.Patrickockander.com

NEW DEFINITIONS:

- "Outlets" will replace most "present-day government systems" Outlets will be places for people to "plug-in" to resources. These outlets will be available to plug in to via Internet and/or physical locations.

- "Perpetual system" ~ Versus present day federalized systems that entangle U.S. in federal webs of bureaucratic barriers to True Freedom. Perpetual systems will streamline and frap the best of what we can salvage of what the government has created, cash infuse it, establish financial Trusts, and assist in getting it running prior to cutting it loose to The People (general public).

Made in the USA
Monee, IL
04 November 2026

67374702R00115